Good News to the Ends of the Earth
The Theology of Acts

Howard Clark Kee

Good News
to the Ends of the Earth

The Theology of Acts

SCM PRESS
London

TRINITY PRESS INTERNATIONAL
Philadelphia

Wingate College Library

First published 1990

SCM Press Ltd
26–30 Tottenham Road
London N1 4BZ

Trinity Press international
3725 Chestnut Street
Philadelphia, Pa. 19104

British Library Cataloguing in Publication Data

Kee, Howard Clark *1920–*
    Good news to the ends of the earth.
    1.   Bible. N. T. Acts – Critical studies
    I.   Title
    226.606

    ISBN 0–334–02486–2

Library of Congress Cataloging-in-Publication Data

Kee, Howard Clark.
    Good news to the ends of the earth: the theology of Acts
    Howard Clark Kee.
        p. cm.
    Includes bibliographical references.
    ISBN 0–334–02486–2
    1.   Bible. N. T. Acts—Theology. I. Title.
BS2625, 5,KA 1990
226.6'06—dc20   90-38163

Phototypeset by Input Typesetting Ltd
and printed in Great Britain by
Clays Ltd, St Ives Plc, Bungay, Suffolk

Contents

1 Perspectives on the Study of Acts   1

2 Jesus as God's Agent for Renewal of His People   6
   1. Jesus as the Fulfilment of the Scriptures   6
   2. God Confirms Jesus and His Followers by Signs
      and Wonders   9
   3. The Roles of Jesus in God's Plan for His New People   10
   4. Present and Future Roles of Jesus   26

3 The Spirit as God's Instrument in the Present Age   28
   1. The Role of the Spirit in the Life of Jesus   28
   2. The Spirit as the Instrument for Launching the
      Good News to the Ends of the Earth   30
   3. The Spirit as Agent of Confirmation of Community
      Membership   35
   4. The Spirit as Agent of Empowerment and Guidance   36
   5. The Spirit as Instrument of Judgment   39

4 Reaching out across Religious and Cultural Boundaries   42
   1. Beginning in Jerusalem   42
   2. The Transition Begins through Peter   50
   3. Wider Outreach: Geographically, Ethnically and
      Culturally   53
   4. Christian Encounter with Graeco-Roman Religion,
      Philosophy and Political Order   60
   5. Mounting Tensions with Civil Authorities and
      Established Cultural Institutions   65

5 Structure and Strategy in the New Community   70
   1. The Leadership Structure   70
   2. Terms for Describing the New Community   81
   3. Life-Style of the New Community   86
   4. Strategy of the New Community   89

6 Witnesses to the Ends of the Earth   95
    1. The Ground and Content of the Witness   95
    2. The Call of the Witnesses   96
    3. The Prototype of the Witnesses in Acts   97
    4. The Commissioning of the Witnesses in Acts   99
    5. The Authority of the Witness   104
    6. The Locus of the Witness and the Witnesses   105

Notes   108

Index of Biblical References   118

1

Perspectives on the Study of Acts

The book of Acts has offered a special challenge to interpreters of the New Testament because it is unique within that body of writings in that it alone tells the story of the two-dimensional growth of the gospel. That is, (1) In personal terms, it describes the movement that was launched by Jesus and was carried forward by his followers and by Paul. (2) In geographical terms, it traces the progress of the gospel from Jerusalem to Rome. The intention of this study of Acts is to perceive the theological import of this story of the spread of the gospel, although such an inquiry must on occasion deal with the question of the historical value of the book as well.

These are by no means new lines of inquiry, although the formulation of the questions about Acts has changed significantly in the latter part of the twentieth century.[1] A century and a half ago, F.C. Baur announced as his "sole purpose" in analysing the New Testament "to comprehend the historically given in its pure objectivity, as far as is generally possible".[2] But in fact, the determinative factor in Baur's historical work was not the historical evidence but the philosophy of Hegel, with its dictum that history moves by the emergence of a principle (thesis) which evokes a counter-principle (antithesis), from which emerges a synthesis. This historical dynamic Baur thought he discerned in Acts, where his theory ran that one wing of the early Christians located Jesus within law-observant Judaism, while the other segment interpreted him in terms of the values and perceptions of the Graeco–Roman world. For Baur, Peter as depicted in Acts represented the former, and Paul the latter. Acts was an effort to overcome these differences and to unite the two opposing wings into a more nearly unified early church.[3] Even though he

1

later characterized Acts as containing "intentional deviations from historical truth",[4] Baur was convinced that what shaped the book of Acts was the development at the end of the first century of what German scholarship came to call "early catholic Christianity" – which represented his Hegel-derived synthesis in both form and substance.

By the end of the nineteenth century, German scholars on the whole took this assessment of Acts as self-evident. Adolf Jülicher asserted that the author of Acts had not consciously set about synthesizing the Pauline and Petrine positions, but – writing in ignorance, with incomplete materials available and lacking the ability to put himself back into the mid-first-century situation – he had blandly assumed that the "early catholicism" of his day was like it had been from the beginning.[5] For Jülicher, the Hegelian synthesis which posited the formation of the early Gentile church created the understanding of Christianity he believed to be present in Acts without the author's consciousness of that thesis/antithesis dynamic. For Baur, on the other hand, Acts was a conscious attempt at synthesis on the part of the writer.

In the ensuing years, and down to the present, analysis of Acts has operated predominantly on the assumption of some sort of dialectic between what are often assumed to be clearly demarcated Jewish and Gentile modes of Christianity. Even though the monumental five-volume study of Acts begun by F.J. Foakes-Jackson and K. Lake in *The Beginnings of Christianity* and continued by H.J. Cadbury[6] provided a wealth of detailed historical and literary evidence for the cultural setting in which Luke-Acts was written, the announced intention of the first volume in this series was to demonstrate how "Christianity in the first century achieved a synthesis between the Greco-Oriental and the Jewish religions in the Roman empire".[7] The Hegelian enterprise was still operative, but as we shall see, the reference to the religious alternatives of the first century as multiple (rather than binary) left open the possibility for a more appropriate analysis of Acts that took into account the great diversity represented within both Judaism and the Graeco-Roman religions of that period. Regrettably however, the dominant factor in the study of Acts has remained the Jew-Gentile dialectic.

Cadbury's important work on the literary and conceptual phenomena of the Roman world in the first century was supplemented by the valuable insights of Martin Dibelius, whose studies of Acts applied to this book the form-critical methods he had developed in his analyses of the gospels. His efforts to distinguish the literary and oral sources used in writing Acts, and his theorizing about the historical methods of this book continue to merit careful attention for understanding Acts.[8] Most important for our purposes but rarely taken into account, however, are Dibelius' declaration that there is no Petrine/Pauline dialectic in Acts, and his insistence that Paul as represented in Acts is not rejecting temple, law or emperor.[9] We shall see that historically it was not only Christianity that had diverse opinions about the need to obey the Law of Moses, but also that there was a range of points of view on basic issues of covenantal identity and obligation among first-century Jews as well.

In 1954 another version of the Baur/Hegel dialectic appeared in Hans Conzelmann's *Die Mitte der Zeit*, which in a few years was translated into English with the prosaic title, *The Theology of St Luke*.[10] Taking his cue from Luke 16:16, Conzelmann developed the theory that Luke was dealing simultaneously with the problem of the delay of the coming of Christ in triumph and with the need to formulate a theological framework in which the ongoing church and its wider mission to the Roman world could be justified. John the Baptist, the theory ran, was the closing figure of (1) the old era, which was the time of Israel, the law and the prophets; (2) Luke's gospel depicted the second era, which was the time of the earthly ministry and death of Jesus; (3) the third era was the time of Jesus' exaltation and the church's mixed experience of mission and testing. This last period would culminate in the triumphant coming of Christ and the final establishment of God's Rule. Appealing as this theory is, and insightful as it is in detail, it shares the basic Baur notion of a radical disjunction between ancient Judaism and emergent Christianity, and assumes a unitary view within Judaism at that time.

In the 1960s, various studies of Luke-Acts contributed illuminating details for understanding these books. Ernst Haenchen's huge commentary on Acts, with its wealth of valuable insights, makes the important point that for Luke the mission to the Gentiles does not lead to a break with Jewish faith. In Acts, as Haenchen read it, the conflicts between the apostles and Jewish leaders are depicted as intra-Jewish disputes, and are so recognized by the Roman authorities.[11] Haenchen notes, however, that the major issue for Acts was how to justify Paul's mission to Gentiles without requiring them to conform to the law – an issue that the author was aware of as a feature of the past, but which he lacked the resources to describe in true historical perspective.[12] Another important volume on Acts published in the 60s was *Studies in Luke-Acts*, edited by L.E. Keck and J.L. Martyn.[13] The essays in this volume cover such themes as christology, the relation of Acts to Paul, literary and historical analyses of Acts (some of which will be referred to below). Most important for our purposes, however, is the charge by Ulrich Wilckens in his essay in this volume that the existentialist theology of post-World War II transmuted Pauline apocalyptic eschatology and soteriology, together with the hope of renewal of the community of faith which that expectation of divine action in human history fostered, into an individualistic mode of experience.[14] One of the chapters in J.A. Fitzmyer's *Luke the Theologian: Aspects of His Teaching* addresses this concern about the individualistic understanding of the gospel in Paul and Acts as well as the false distinctions that are made between Judaism and Christianity in the first century. His analysis of this issue appears in his chapter titled "The Jewish People and the Mosaic Law in Luke-Acts". In spite of such important critiques of the older scholarly position, the Baur-Hegelian construct of "early catholicism" as a major factor in shaping Acts has continued to have its exponents, as is apparent in E. Käsemann's essay on "Paul and Early Catholicism" in his *New Testament Questions of Today*.[15]

It is only in the past decade and a half that due attention has been paid by historians of Second Temple Judaism and the origins of Christianity to the question of covenantal participation as a central issue for both Judaism and early Christianity. The diversity of answers to this question is highlighted in the choice of title for a collection of essays edited by Jacob Neusner and colleagues: *Judaisms and Their Messiahs*.[16] Thus the importance attached by Fitzmyer to the definition of community in Luke-Acts, as referred to above, is a significant part of growing scholarly attention to the factor of different modes of covenantal identity and developing approaches for dealing with this issue in the study of the New Testament as a whole.[17] Useful literary and thematic analyses of Acts were also published in the 1970s and 80s, many of them through the Luke-Acts Group of the Society of Biblical Literature.[18] Also recently, in a movement influenced by liberation theology, essays have been published which treat the political dimensions of Luke-Acts.[19]

Other recent studies, written from a variety of perspectives, have begun to address the issue of the relationship of the church to Israel. A pioneer work on this theme was that of Jacob Jervell, *Luke and the People of God*.[20] An important monograph which builds effectively on sociological insights to discern the intention of Luke and the dynamics of the community he addresses is P.F. Esler's *Community and Gospel in Luke-Acts: The Social and Political Motivations of Lucan Theology*.[21]

What is required in the study of the theology of Acts, therefore, is to drawn upon the insights about the social, political, literary and cultural setting of the Roman world in which the early church was living and working.[22] But at the same time it is essential to examine the fluid and varied answers to the widespread and urgent question among Jews as to what constituted their identity as the heirs to God's covenantal promises and as those addressed by God through the legal and prophetic traditions of ancient Israel. The persistent notion that Acts is concerned to synthesize "Judaism" and early "Christianity" – a heritage from Baur – ignores the fact that both those nouns refer to concurrent processes within widely varied religious developments in the first and second centuries rather than to clearly defined entities. One has only to reflect for a moment on the factors which differentiated Sadducees, Pharisees and Essenes from each other on the issue of covenantal participation to see how significantly different *Judaisms* were in this period from the emergent Jewish orthodoxy that subsequently legitimated itself in the Mishnah and Talmud – writings created in the period from the second to the sixth century of the Common Era.[23]

In our analysis of Acts, we shall also take into account the variety of ways in which Jews of this period described the agent – or agents – of God through whom the divine purpose for his people was to be accomplished. It is the aim of this study of the theology of Acts to discern the distinctive features of defining participation in the covenant and the messianic role in this book, and to see how these factors shape the attitudes toward politics, culture, ethics and other religious traditions expressed therein.

2

Jesus as God's Agent for Renewal of His People

1. Jesus as the Fulfilment of the Scriptures

In the Gospel of Luke, there is voiced the repeated claim that what Jesus has said and done is in fulfilment of the scriptures. Clearly for the author of Acts "fulfilment" is not a matter of theological mathematics, as though one item in the Jewish scriptures was the obvious equivalent of something done or said by Jesus and the apostles. Fulfilment is a dynamic process, with many variants, but the common element between promise and fulfilment for Luke and Acts is the accomplishment of God's purpose for his people and through them for the world. In some cases the link is one of symbolic parallel. Thus fulfilment is implicit in the stories of the birth of John the Baptist and Jesus, which parallel those of the birth of Samuel,[1] whose major task was to prepare for the accession to the throne of Israel's king, just as John's primary role is that of preparer for Jesus as the divinely chosen and endowed agent of the coming Kingdom of God. But it becomes explicit at two crucial points in Luke's account of Jesus: (1) at the synagogue in Nazareth, where Jesus directly claims that the work that he is launching is in fulfilment of scripture (Luke 4:16–21; cf. Isa. 61:1–2) and when he points to the parallel between his reaching out to heal Gentiles and the precedents set by the prophets Elijah and Elisha (Luke 4:25–28; cf. I Kings 17:1; 18:1–2; 17:8–9; II Kings 5:14). The most direct and comprehensive claim made by Jesus in Luke appears in his instruction to the disciples after

6

his resurrection (Luke 24:26–27, 44), where he declares that his sufferings were a necessary stage in his role as messiah, and documents this claim from "Moses and all the prophets". The subsequent statement is even more sweeping in its assertion that all three of the sections of the Jewish Bible (law, prophets, psalms) point to Jesus, his suffering, his resurrection, the message of forgiveness, and the universal outreach of the gospel. Far from there being any suggestion that God's purpose for his people as announced in the Jewish scriptures has been supplanted, Luke represents Jesus as declaring that what has been God's announced plan through-out the history of Israel is now to come to fruition through the world-wide mission of the church.

For the author of Acts, the resurrection of Jesus is far more than the resuscitation of a corpse. It is the fulfilment of promises uttered by the psalmist that God will exalt to his right hand his chosen instrument, enabling him to escape death and bodily decay, granting him renewed life in God's presence, and triumphing over his enemies (Acts 2:25–28, 34–35; cf. Ps. 16:8–11; Ps. 110:1). Adding to the traditional attribution of the psalms to David, Acts reports Peter as calling David a prophet as well (2:29–31). Themes from the psalms appear in Paul's sermons as well. In his address to the synagogue in Pisidian Antioch Paul declares that God's having raised Jesus from the dead fulfills "what God promised to the fathers" (13:32). He then proceeds to quote from the psalms and the prophet Isaiah to show that God's plan from the outset was to raise from the dead his chosen instrument (13:33–35; cf. Ps. 2:7; Isa. 55:3; Ps. 16:10).

Equally as important as the claims about the fulfilment of scripture on specific points is the way in which Acts depicts the apostles as placing what God has done through and for Jesus in the larger context of the history of Israel. The sermon in Antioch begins with a summary account of God's having chosen and guided the patriarchs, destroyed their enemies to enable his people to take over the land of Canaan. The climax came when God established his rule over his people through David the king, whose heir Jesus is (13:16–23). At the same time, there is to be no surprise that many in Israel in the days of the apostles reject this message from God about Jesus and the destiny of his people. The prophet had foreseen that there would be unbelief even though God performed a most spectacular act in their midst (13:40–41; cf. Hab. 1:5).

From the standpoint of most first-century Jewish messianic hopes, the most problematical dimension of the Christians' claim that Jesus was God's agent was the tradition that in fulfilment of this divinely-ordained role he had experienced rejection, suffering and death. Although the book of Daniel makes the point repeatedly in its stories that the faithful remnant of Israel must be prepared to suffer and even to die in the time of struggle before God's final triumph over the powers of evil, there is in that apocalyptic writing no developed doctrine of a suffering messiah. In Peter's address to the crowd in the temple portico (3:18), he notes that "God had foretold by the mouth of all the prophets that his Messiah should suffer", but he does not quote any prophetic texts. Even in the Suffering Servant section of Isaiah (Isa. 52:13–53:12), it is not clear whether the prophet was envisioning an individual or a faithful group whose suffering would have redemptive value for others. Clearly, in Isa. 41:8–10 it is corporate Israel that is addressed as Yahweh's servant, just as in Daniel the "one like a son of man" to whom God gives the kingdom (Dan. 7:13–14) is the community of the saints (7:18, 22). In Acts 3:13, however, the term translated "servant" (*pais*) in the Septuagintal version of Isa. 52:13 is not used with reference to Jesus' suffering, but expresses rather his special relationship to God: "child" (cf. also Acts 3:26; 4:27, 30). The single place in Acts where Isaiah 53 is directly quoted (8:32–33) makes no direct reference to Jesus as suffering servant, although it does emphasize his role as a sacrificial lamb.

Therefore we may infer that for the author of Acts and his readers there was no developed, traditional image of a suffering messiah which would be recognized by Jewish students of scripture in the first century and which therefore could be assigned to Jesus. Yet the death of Jesus is said in Acts to have been foreseen in scripture as the outcome of a coalition of evil powers – Gentile and Jewish – who were hostile toward the one who had been chosen and empowered by God, as the quotation from Ps. 2:1–2 in Acts 4:25–26 makes dramatically clear. In this context Jesus is explicitly referred to as God's Anointed, as well as the "child" of the Lord (4:27). For the author of Acts, therefore, there is in the scriptures no neatly defined messianic role which is to be assigned to Jesus, but there is a whole series of redemptive functions which the discerning eye can perceive in the scriptures and which Jesus has fulfilled.

2. God Confirms Jesus and His Followers by Signs and Wonders

That Jesus has fulfilled these divinely prescribed redemptive roles is not only confirmed in retrospect by a careful reading of the scriptures, but has been further attested by events in the recent past, as the author of Acts notes. Chief among these confirmatory factors is his having been raised from the dead. That this event occurred the apostles attest on the basis of their extended association with the risen Lord (Acts 1:2–3). To have been a witness of Jesus' resurrection, as well as of his earthly career, was an indispensable requirement for apostleship (1:21–22), as Peter reaffirmed in his Pentecost sermon (2:32), and as Paul declared in his sermon in Antioch (13:30).

In addition to the testimony of those who had seen Jesus risen from the dead, Acts draws repeated attention to the miracles which were performed by Jesus or in his name by his followers as confirmation of what they were claiming about him. Even the occurrence of such miraculous signs was foretold in the scriptures, according to Acts (2:19; cf. Joel 2:28–30), and the "mighty works, signs and wonders" of Jesus are accordingly noted (2:23). Furthermore, the performance of signs by the apostles is in direct continuity with those done by Jesus (2:43). The healing of the man in the portico of Solomon is attributed to faith in Jesus (3:16), as even the official opponents of the apostles acknowledge (4:16–18). The people of Jerusalem, however, praise God as the one ultimately responsible for the healing of the lame man in the temple (4:21). In the common prayer of the apostles reported in Acts 4:24–31 there is an appeal that God will continue to manifest his power and reinforce the gospel message through healings which they will be enabled to do in the name of Jesus. This does in fact occur in the Acts narrative, as signs and wonders are performed through the apostles, and many sick and lame and demon-possessed are brought to them and find healing. Indeed, the claim is made that "they were all healed" (5:12–16).

Stephen, one of the Greek-speaking leaders chosen by the apostles (6:1–6), is described as having done "great signs and wonders among the people" (6:8). So significant and appealing is that aspect of the work of the apostles and their co-workers that through these miracles multitudes come to believe the message "when they . . . saw the signs" (8:6), and indeed many are healed or freed from demon-possession (8:7). So successful is this healing activity that Simon the magician tries to purchase the power (8:9–24). The confirmatory function of these signs is noted in Acts 14, where the success at the apostles evokes hostility from their opponents at Iconium (14:1–7) but at Lystra results in mass acclaim of Paul and Barnabas as gods in disguise (14:8–18). When Paul and Barnabas confer with the apostolic circle in Jerusalem, the confirmatory force of the miracles done through these two messengers to the Gentiles is seen as confirming the validity of the mission to the non-Jewish world (15:12). We shall examine in Chapters 3 and 4 how God is seen at work through the apostles to bring the gospel and participation in the new community to a world-wide audience.

3. The Roles of Jesus in God's Plan for His New People

We have noted that Acts in describing what Jesus has done to fulfil God's purpose for his people does not simply apply to Jesus' traditional messianic titles or roles. Indeed, the Jewish scriptures do not offer sharply defined messianic categories. Instead, Acts depicts or designates Jesus in a wide range of functions and with a diversity of titles in his work as God's redemptive agent. Some of these are familiar from both Jewish and early Christian sources, while others are less common or even distinctively Lukan. Some are linked directly with the term, Messiah, while others have importantly different titles, and some roles rather than titles. We shall examine how the author of Acts uses both the traditional messianic designations and how he includes others not found elsewhere in Jewish or early Christian literature.

3.1 Christ/Messiah

As we have just noted, there was in Judaism at the turn of the eras no uniform understanding of Messiah. The general view was of a commissioned, empowered agent of God, whose role was to achieve a liberating or renewing role for God's covenant people. As is evident from both the later Jewish scriptures and the Dead Sea writings, the Anointed One could fulfil either a royal or priestly function. As is evident from the Dead Sea Scrolls, there was more than one messiah expected, as in the prediction of the Messiah of Aaron and the Messiah of Israel in *The Messianic Rule* (1QSa), where the priestly messiah has priority over the royal figure. In the *Messianic Anthology* (4Q175), there are three figures expected in the end-time: a prophet (in fulfilment of Deut. 18:18–19), a royal and a priestly messiah. The messianic roles range from announcing the coming of the end of the age through exercise of royal authority to purification of God's people in the new age. There was no single, broadly agreed-upon definition of what Messiah was to do, any more than there was a single title or even set of terms for describing the task of the agent of God who was to prepare his people for the new age. The interpreter of Acts must examine the messianic and related terms that are used in the immediate context in which they appear in order to determine their specific connotations.

The traditional title, Christ/Messiah, is applied to Jesus by Peter in the address on the day of Pentecost in connection with God having raised him from the dead (2:31). The resurrection is represented as not merely triumph over death or as assurance of the deliverance of the faithful from death, as in Paul's account in I Cor. 15:20. Here in Acts its significance is the exaltation of Jesus to the place of honor at the right hand of God (2:32–36). In fulfilment of Ps. 110:1, Jesus has been made "both Lord and Christ", this one "whom you [the religious leaders] crucified". The future role of Jesus as "the Christ" is also defined by Peter in his sermon in the temple portico (3:18–20), where the prophetic predictions of the sufferings of the Messiah are mentioned (though not quoted). Unusual is the declaration that – in the future – God will send "the Messiah appointed for you", who is Jesus. The prayer of the gathered community in Jerusalem, following the release of Peter and John by the Jewish authorities (4:1–22), includes a quotation from Psalm 2, where there is a description of the coalition of Gentiles and rulers against "the Lord and his anointed" (4:25–26). In the Psalm quoted, the problem is that nations surrounding Israel have formed a coalition to dethrone or kill the king of Israel, who is viewed as having been chosen and empowered by Yahweh. What is promised in the psalm is a reversal of results, in that Israel's enemies will be smashed by the combined efforts of God and his chosen ruler (Ps. 2:8–9). The special relationship of the king to Yahweh is indicated under the figure of the monarch as God's son (2:7). For the author of Acts, however, the one who is God's son and king-designate is identified as Jesus, whom God anointed for his salvific role in behalf of God's people (4:27), who had been executed through the combined efforts of "Herod and Pontius Pilate, with the Gentiles and the people of Israel". That God had anointed and therefore chosen, commissioned and empowered Jesus is now publicly discernible through the signs and wonders that are being performed in his name.

This identification of Jesus as the one anointed by God matches well with the claim of Jesus made explicitly by him in Luke's unique version of the gospel story of his address to the synagogue in Nazareth. There the promise of the anointing – one might without great distortion of intent translate this word as "messiahing" – by the Spirit given in Isa. 61 is declared by Jesus to be in process of fulfilment through him (Luke 4:16–21). In that quotation, as is the case throughout Acts, the emphasis on Jesus as messiah falls more on the functional factor of what he does in fulfilment of God's purpose than on the personal or substantive question of who he is in relation to God, as was later to be spelled out in the creeds, in Peter's address at the home of the Roman centurion, Cornelius. This estimate of Jesus is the one that is expressed clearly by Peter in his address at the home of the Roman centurion, Cornelius (10:34–43) when he surveys what Jesus did in his capacity as anointed by the Holy Spirit. It is God who is the ultimate source of redemptive activity in the world, even to "preaching the good news of peace by Jesus Christ". It was God who "anointed Jesus of Nazareth with the Holy Spirit and with power" so that he could fulfil his ministry of good works, of healing, and of exorcisms. The crucial factor was that "God was with him", and had empowered him to carry out his role in the divine purpose.

3.2 Son of Man

The titles linked with Jesus' messianic role in the synoptic tradition are relatively rare in Acts. The Son of Man, referred to 24 times in Luke's gospel – 10 of which are unique to Luke – is found only once in Acts. Luke draws upon both Mark and Q for his Son of Man sayings, but adds several that are unique to his gospel. Six of the Son of Man sayings in this gospel describe the present role of Jesus as Son of Man: (1) a figure of authority to forgive sins (9:58), as Lord of the sabbath (6:5), violating social and dietary restrictions about eating (7:34); (2) experiencing rejection and betrayal (9:58; 22:48[2]); (3) one whose mission is to save the lost (19:10). There are references to his suffering and death as Son of Man, building on the Markan tradition (9:22, 44). The overwhelming preponderance of references in Luke to the Son of Man, however, are to his future role as judge: 6:22[3]; 9:26; 12:8; 12:10; 12:40; 17:22, 24, 26, 30; 18:8; 21:27, 36[4]. Since most of the Son of Man sayings in Luke (and especially in his distinctive passages) picture him as coming Son of Man and/or judge, it is not surprising that in the single occurrence of the term in Acts (7:56), the figure of Jesus seen by Stephen in a vision just before his martyr death is as the Son of Man installed in his role of power beside God in the heavens.

There is an additional feature of the Son of Man sayings in the Gospel of Luke which serves to support the view of God's directing human history as it is represented in Acts. Luke expands the prediction of the passion in Mark 10:33 to include the declaration that "everything written of the Son of Man by the prophets will be accomplished" (18:31). In anticipation of his trial and death, Jesus says in Luke's passion narrative that "the Son of Man goes as it has been determined [by God]" (Luke 22:22). Luke alters the next to the last verse of Mark (16:7) to recall that Jesus had told his followers in Galilee of the arrest, crucifixion and resurrection of the Son of Man (Luke 24:26). This fits with Luke's scheme in Acts, where the disciples are not to return to Galilee but to remain in Jerusalem. Equally significant for Luke's linking the gospel evidence with his depiction of the apostles in Jerusalem and the visions of the risen Christ that are granted Paul and Stephen is the slight alteration of Mark 14:62 from a future reference to the exalted Jesus to the distinctive Lukan promise that *"From now on the Son of Man will be seated at the right hand of power"* (22:69). As a follow up to this in Acts, no title could be more appropriate for Stephen to use in identifying the one he sees at God's right hand than "the Son of Man".

3.3 Son of God

Son of God is less frequently used than Son of Man in Luke's gospel,[5] although Luke has inserted the phrase in three places: (1) in his version of Mark's summary account of Jesus' healings and exorcisms (4:41; cf. Mark 1:32–34); (2) in the annunciation by Gabriel of Jesus' birth (1:32); and (3) in the scene depicting the trial of Jesus (22:70). In each of these occurrences, the import of the phrase is that Jesus stands in a special relationship with God, as evident in the unique powers which are at work through him. In Acts 9:20, Paul's message to the synagogues in Damascus is epitomized in the simple declaration: Jesus is the Son of God. In 13:26–39, however, the argument of Paul from scripture identifying Jesus as Son of God involves an amazing synthesis of what might seem to be disparate texts, as analysis of the Pauline exegesis in this sermon shows.

After asserting that God raised Jesus from the dead and that he was visible to many witnesses over an extended period of time, Paul declares that what has happened is the fulfilment of "what God promised to the fathers". The argument consists of the exegesis of passages from the psalms and the prophets. The first text quoted[6] is from an enthronement psalm (Ps. 2:7) in which God addresses the king of Israel as his son and designates him as the one whom he begot that day. Having established the sonship of Jesus, the next step in the argument affirms that God will give to this son the – unspecified – "holy and sure mercies of David", using a text from Isa. 55:3.[7] The link in this network of scriptures is David as the ancestor of Jesus and the prototype of Israel's ultimate king. The final step in the argument derives from Ps. 16:10 (LXX) where God's promise that his Holy One will not see corruption is changed from an expression of gratitude that the psalmist's life has been preserved so that he could enjoy life in the presence of God to the declaration that it has been fulfilled through Jesus' having been delivered from death. The point is made that David himself did not enjoy God's presence forever, but that Jesus, David's descendant, has been enabled by God to share in the resurrection from the dead (13:38). It is this event which demonstrates that Jesus is the Son of God to whom this configuration of scriptures point.

3.4 Son of David

The use of the title, Son of David and the link of Jesus with his Davidic ancestry are important features in Luke's gospel. Prominent in the infancy narratives are the mention of Joseph's descent from the line of David (1:27) and the report that just before his birth the family of Jesus went to their ancestral town, Bethlehem, in order to enroll in the census required by Caesar. Lest the reader miss the point, Luke adds that Joseph was "of the house and lineage of David" (2:4). The report to the shepherds of the birth of Jesus locates that event "in the city of David" (2:11). Jesus' genealogy is traced through David (3:31). Luke also reproduces the Markan accounts of Jesus' having been addressed as "Son of David" by the blind beggar near Jericho (Mark 10:47–48; Luke 18:38–39), and Jesus' appeal to the precedent of David for his violation of the law by plucking grain on the sabbath (Mark 2:23:28; Luke 6:1–5). And in the accounts of Jesus' controversies with the Jewish leaders just before his arrest and crucifixion (Mark 12:35–37; Luke 20:41–44) the affirmation is recorded that the Messiah is not only Son of David but is also David's Lord, based on the quotation of Ps. 110:1. As we shall see, the question posed by Jesus that is unanswered in Mark or Matthew, "David himself calls [the Messiah] Lord; so how is he his son?" is given an answer in Acts. In his gospel as a whole, Luke is content to stress the continuity between Jesus and David geneaologically, in terms of heritage, in attitude toward the law, and above all in fulfilment of God's purpose for his people.

It is the more striking, therefore, that the title, Son of David, is not used in Acts. Yet at many crucial points in this book the appeal to scripture for understanding and justifying what is happening through Jesus involves David either explicitly or implicitly through quotations from the Psalms. Judas, the defector, is replaced and he is condemned by appeal to two of the psalms (Acts 1:20; cf. Ps. 69:25; 109:8). In the first of these passages, "David", the traditional author of the psalms prays that the enemies of God and his people will lose their habitation. In Acts this is interpreted to mean that the soul will be expelled from the body when the entrails gush out of it and the body is left uninhabited. In the Hebrew text of Ps. 109:8, another imprecatory psalm, the prayer is that the goods of the enemy may be seized by someone else. But is the LXX, quoted

in Acts, what is to be lost by the enemy is his position =
episkopos. Hence, an appeal to David explains the horrible
death of Judas here depicted and his replacement in the
apostolic office. It is these predictions which are said to have
been spoken beforehand by the mouth of David (Acts 1:16).

Central to the main argument of Peter's Pentecost address
is the claim that the resurrection and exaltation of Jesus by
God were predicted by David (2:25–28; Ps. 132:11). The point
is made repeatedly that in these psalms David was not speaking
of himself, since he died and the location of his tomb is still
known. Instead, David is portrayed in Acts not so much as a
prototype of the eschatological king but as a prophet who
foresaw that one of his descendants would ascend this glorious
throne as promised by God. But David himself did not ascend
to heaven, even though he predicted that the Lord of heaven
would give the place of special honor at his right hand to "my
[= David's] Lord". Obviously, "Lord" is not the equivalent of
Yahweh (Lord), but the agent of God through whom God's
sovereign purpose for the creation and for the covenant people
is to be accomplished. In Acts Peter makes the explicit assertion
that this one who is Lord and Messiah, in fulfilment of the
psalm of David, is the same Jesus who was crucified and raised
by God from the dead (2:34–36). The coalition of Jewish and
Gentile leaders which formed "against the Lord and his
anointed" to put him to death accomplished their evil goal in
fulfilment of the words of David (Ps. 2:1–2). All that they did
carried out whatever God's hand and plan "had predestined
to take place" (4:23–28).

Similarly, in Paul's sermon in Pisidian Antioch, there is a
recounting of God's having chosen and prepared Israel and
its leaders for their covenant relationship with God as his
people, culminating in his choice of David to be king (13:16–22).
David is portrayed here as the one after God's heart, "who
will do all my will", a theme which echoes Ps. 89:20 and I Sam.
13:14. The resurrection of Jesus from the dead is in fulfilment
of the promises to David in which the king is acclaimed
as God's son (13:33; cf. Ps. 2:7) and there is assurance of
deliverance of this his chosen instrument from the corruption
of death (13:35; cf. Ps. 16:10). Paul now declares that through
Jesus have been fulfilled the prophetic promises uttered
through Second Isaiah, "I will give you the holy and sure
mercies of David" (13:35; cf. Isa. 55:3). These promises were not

fulfilled for David himself, since he died and "saw corruption" (13:35). It is for and through Jesus that the prophetic announcements have come to pass. Their fulfilment takes place, not through the recovery of a glorious past of national independence presided over by a powerful monarch ruling in Jerusalem and supervising the temple and its cultus through the priesthood, but a truly glorious future in which Jesus is at God's right hand in the presence of God and the sovereignty of his rule is worldwide. The crucial agent in the fulfilment of this universal goal is already in the appropriate place: in the place of honor and power beside God.

Although the apostles, including Paul, are pictured in Acts as taking part in the temple worship, and even though the building of this habitation for God was decided on in the time of David and carried out by his son, Solomon, Stephen's speech culminates in a quotation from Second Isaiah which calls into question the very idea that humans can build a dwelling place for God (Isa. 66:1–2). There is no depiction of the construction of a grander temple than that of Herod, as pictured in the Temple Scroll from Qumran. There is no need for a symbolic structure for God's presence among his people, and it would be wholly inappropriate in the new order of things for it to be given a physical, geographical location on earth. The visions of God, which are confirmed and illuminated by the new understanding of the psalms of David, show where God is and how Jesus has been exalted by God to a place of honor and power. It is in terms of this insight that in Acts 15, when Paul and Barnabas report to the apostles in Jerusalem "what signs and wonders God had done through them among the Gentiles" (15:12), James responds by quoting Amos 9:11–12, which promises the rebuilding of the *skene* of David (Acts 15:16–18). This term could conceivably refer to the booth, or the dwelling, or to the royal house of David, but the point of the promise according to Acts is that through a new structure built on the promises made through David all humanity – including the Gentiles – will seek the Lord. The old structure has fallen, whether the Davidic monarchy or the temple is intended in the prophetic oracle. The point of these quotations is to show (1) that God has not abandoned his promises to Israel through the prophets and the psalms as well as the history of this people, but (2) that the fulfilment of these promises transforms, renews and widens on a potentially universal scale the possibility of participation in the new structure of relationship between God and his new people. David, the idealized king of past history, did not survive to share in the realization of the divine promises which are taking place through Jesus and the new community which he is calling into being.

Another important Davidic text for filling out the Acts picture of Jesus is the quotation from Ps. 118:22 in Acts 4:10 concerning the stone rejected by the builders which has become the head of the corner[8]. At a hearing before the "rulers, elders and scribes" and members of the high priestly family, Peter is moved by the Holy Spirit to raise for the religious leaders of Israel the question as to what the source of power is through which he and the other apostles are able to heal the lame man (Acts 3). The supremely ironic answer was that the instrument of divine power was the person in whose death they had participated through their rejection of Jesus as agent of God. The transformation of the rejected one into his central role in the rebuilding of God's people had been announced long beforehand by David in Psalm 118. The importance of this text from the Davidic tradition for Luke is evident in the account given in his gospel of the Parable of the Wicked Tenants (20:9–19; cf. Mark 12:1–12; Matt. 21:33–46). At the conclusion of the parable, all three synoptic versions quote from Ps. 118 about the rejected stone which has become the head of the corner. Luke omits the next verse which asserts that this is the Lord's doing, but he adds the declaration: "everyone who falls on that stone will be broken to pieces; but when it falls on anyone it will crush him." This heightens the judgmental force of the quote from the psalm, but avoids any direct indication at this point as to who the ultimate agent is who will bring judgment on those who reject his chosen instrument for building the new structure. In Acts 4:10–11, however, it is affirmed that God raised Jesus from the dead, and this the rejection of him by "you builders" (= the Jewish leaders) has led to the new situation in which the name of Jesus is the sole basis of salvation for all humanity.

In this same chapter Acts reports the group prayer (4:24–31), throughout which the emphasis is on the divine sovereignty which encompasses all the natural features of the universe as well as the movement of historical peoples, including Israel, the Gentiles and their leaders. It was God who announced in advance "by the mouth of our father, David," who was God's servant,[9] that there would be a coalition of opponents to the agent of God. This prediction was fulfilled, it is asserted through the convergence of schemes by the Jewish and Roman leaders who would falsely assume that they could destroy Jesus. Yet what they would carry out in their plot against him, motivated by what they assumed to be their own initiative and their own interests would in fact accomplish God's redemptive purpose for his people and for the world. Like David before him, Jesus is God's "servant" (Acts 4:30). Through both of them God works simultaneously to proclaim and to accomplish his purpose: David as prototypical king and Jesus as the unique instrument of the achievement of God's purpose for his people. It is in this sense of continuity between promise and fulfilment that Acts depicts Jesus as "son of David".

3.5 Lord

The term "Lord" (kurios) occurs more than fifty times in Acts. In more than one third of the cases, the title is a designation for God. In nearly half the other occurrences, it is Jesus who is designated as Lord. In the remainder, it is more difficult to determine whether it is Jesus or God who is meant by this term, although most of these passages seem to use "Lord" as equivalent to God.

The emphasis throughout Acts in those passages where Lord=God is on the divine plan for the renewal of God's people through Jesus, in spite of the opposition from the political and religious leaders. In 1:24 God is petitioned to determine who is to join the leadership of the new community by guiding the choice of the one who would succeed Judas in the circle of the twelve apostles. Peter concludes his address on the day of Pentecost with an appeal to all who are called by God the Lord to be part of his people: they must respond through repentance and the acceptance of baptism (2:39). It is the Lord God who raised up Jesus as the prophet promised to Moses and sent him into the world to guide his people (3:19–22), just as the Lord appeared to Moses on Mount Sinai when the old covenant was established with Israel (7:31–33). It is the Lord God who has acted to renew and heal humanity in spite of the human opposition to his new purpose for the world through Jesus (4:26, 29–30). And it is he who will bring under judgment those who exploit or pervert the gifts he gives to his people, as Ananias and Sapphira as well as Simon the sorcerer learn (5:9; 8:24).

It is God the Lord who guides the journeys of his messengers, as in the case of the miraculous transport of Philip from his desert encounter with the Ethiopian eunuch to Ashdod (Azotus; 8:39). It is the Lord and his angels who prepare both Cornelius and Peter for this precedent-setting situation in which the gospel is proclaimed to a Roman military officer and his household described in Acts 10 (cf. 10:4, 33). The launching of the mission to the Gentiles is commanded by the Lord God (13:47) and confirmed by a quotation from his prophet (Isa. 49:6). The apostles assembled in Jerusalem come to the realization, articulated by James, that it is the non-Israelite segment of humanity who are now seeking the Lord. This dramatic new development is not a random occurrence, but is rather the fulfilment of what has been declared by the Lord through the prophets (15:13–18; cf. Amos 9:11–12; Jer. 12:15; Isa. 45:21)[10].

There are in Acts at least ten passages where Lord could be understood as referring either to God or to Jesus. In 2:47 it is probably God who is said to have added to the number of his people those who were being saved, just as in 21:14 Paul's prayer that the Lord's will might be done is likely addressed to God. Somewhat less certain references to God are the notes (1) that the churches in the various parts of Palestine "walked in fear of the Lord" (12:11, 17), (2) that "the Lord" sent an angel to free Peter from prison (12:11, 17), and (3) that Herod Antipas was struck dead by an angel of the Lord (12:23). What seem to be more likely references to Jesus as Lord occur in 7:60, where Stephen prays for forgiveness for his executioners; in 13:2, where the church at Antioch in Syria worships "the Lord"; in 16:14–15, and where "the Lord" opens Lydia's heart to hear Paul's message and she responds by seeking to be faithful to "the Lord".

Throughout Acts, however, there are unambiguous references to Jesus as the Lord. The witnesses of his earthly career are those "who went in and out with the Lord Jesus" (1:21). Teachings of "the Lord Jesus" not found in the gospel tradition are quoted by Paul in Acts 20:35, where the saying, "It is more blessed to give than to receive" is explicitly identified in the phrase of Paul calling his hearers to "remember the words of the Lord Jesus". Both the encounter with the risen Lord (1:6) and the appeal to that experience of him (4:33) are mentioned in Acts, as are the visions of him raised to God's right hand (2:25, 34). Stephen is reported to have seen Jesus in this exalted position (7:59), and Paul is confronted by Jesus as the risen Lord (9:10–11, 13, 15, 17; 18:9). The proclamation of the gospel in Acts calls for the hearers to turn to or to believe in the Lord (5:14; 9:35; 11:17), and the believers are called to remain faithful "to the Lord" (11:24). They are referred to as "disciples of the Lord" (9:1). It is the Lord who is the subject of the teaching which the apostles undertake in Acts and which results in the conversion of the hearers (13:12; 14:3; 23:11; 28:31). They are called to serve the Lord (20:19). It is from the Lord that they receive their ministry (20:24), and it is for him that they are to be ready to die (21:13).

To acknowledge Jesus as Lord is the basic confession of the church, according to Acts (10:26; 11:16; 16:31; 20:21), just as he is the subject of the preaching of the apostles. With no effort to define the relationship of Jesus to God, the author of Acts uses the title, Lord, to refer to them both. In this way he implies the intimate interconnection between who Jesus is, what he does, and how these factors achieve God's redemptive purpose for and through his new people. There are here no hints of the later concern for specification of the relation of the divine to the human in Jesus, to say nothing of speculation about whether there was a divine nature of Jesus which was eternal or bestowed in time. There is continuity between the redemptive purpose of God and the salvific work of Jesus, so that the traditional term, Lord, can be applied to either or both.

3.6 Distinctive Titles of Jesus in Acts

Jesus is designated four times in the opening chapters of Acts as *pais* (3:13, 26; 4:27, 30). In Peter's address in the temple portico, as in the apostle's prayer, this term – usually translated "servant" – is linked with the suffering and exaltation of Jesus. In the LXX, *pais* is used to translate the Hebrew *ebed* in about half the passages where the term occurs.[11] From the contexts in which the word appears it is evident that the references are to different persons in different writings. At times *pais* is a self-designation of the person or group seen to be righteous before God. This may include the whole of Israel, or a faithful remnant. Elsewhere "servant" is a depiction of an important figure in Israel's history: the patriarchs, Moses, the king, a prophet, or Job. In Second Isaiah, the term is applied in some cases to the faithful community within ethnic Israel, but elsewhere in those prophetic pronouncements it is used of a chosen instrument of God, apparently an individual (Isa. 42:1; 49:3). His role is to bring justice to God's people (52:13; 53:11), which involves setting things right between them and God (42:1–4). The outcome of what he will do is that the blind will receive sight (42:7), darkness will be dispelled (49:9), people will come to know God (44:22), and the light of God will shine upon the nations (49:5). His God-given task will be accomplished through suffering (52:13–53:12). As we saw to be the case with the title, Son of Man, "servant" in the Old Testament alternates between an individual and a group reference, thereby dramatizing the interconnections between the destiny of God's agent and God's covenant people. In Luke 1:54 and 69 the nation Israel and king David are referred to as "servant". The only other gospel context where the servant motif of Second Isaiah appears explicitly (Matt. 12:15–21) is a description of Jesus' healing activity, of the outpouring of the Spirit through him, and his outreach to the Gentiles to proclaim justice and bring them hope. This blend of connotations of servant – as agent of God and metaphor for God's people – is evident in Acts as well, where Jesus' death and resurrection are essential to God's plan for the renewal of the covenant community.

Associated with Jesus as God's servant in Acts (3:26) is the claim expressed by Peter that Jesus is the prophet whose coming was foretold by Moses (3:20–23; cf. Deut. 18:15–19). The point is made in this passage in Acts that God has raised up Jesus as the ultimate prophet, and that those who do not listen to him will be cut off from God's people. This warning is offered against the background of the declaration that the people of Israel are the children and heirs of those to whom God gave the covenantal promises, including Abraham, who was told that in him all the families of the earth would be blessed (3:24–26; cf. Gen. 22:18). The association of Jesus with the role of prophet is found in various places throughout the synoptic tradition. Jesus implies that his rejection in his hometown is the expected fate of a prophet (Mark 6:4 = Matt. 13:57), and he is associated with the prophets in popular evaluation of his healings and pronouncements (Mark 6:15; Luke 9:8). His disciples report this estimate of him when he asks who people are saying that he is (Mark 8:28 = Matt. 16:14), but Luke expands this description to have the observers declare, "One of the prophets has arisen" (Luke 9:19). This reflects the belief found in the Qumran and John the Baptist traditions, which build on Deut. 18:15–18 and Malachi 5:5–6 to declare that an eschatological prophet has been sent by God to renew the covenant people. The prototypes of these prophets of the last days may be Moses or Elijah. Jesus' prophetic role is further indicated in several unique Lukan passages: in response to the healing of the widow's son (7:16): in his reaction to the warning of the Pharisees about Herod's aim to kill him (13:33); in the final words of the account of the rich man and Lazarus, where the words of Moses and the prophets are linked with Jesus' rising from the dead (16:31). In the first encounter between the disciples and the risen Jesus, they declare him to have been "a prophet mighty in word and deed before God and all the people" (24:19). The stage is set, therefore, for Peter's identification of Jesus as the prophet promised by Moses, as noted above, although Acts adds to the text from Deuteronomy the warning of destruction upon those who do not heed his message (perhaps under the influence of Lev. 23:29). This motif of the rejection of the prophet whom God promised to Moses is repeated in Acts 7:37, as a part of Stephen's warning to Israel about the consequences of neglecting Jesus and what God is declaring to his people through him. The precedent for their killing God's prophets is recalled by Stephen in 7:52. The rejection of Jesus by the Jewish leaders and his having been raised from the dead are declared by Paul in his defense before King Agrippa to have been foretold by "Moses and the prophets", who also announced that this first one to rise from the dead "would proclaim light both to the people [Israel] and to the Gentiles" (26:21–23). Although there are other passages in the New Testament which link Jesus to the role of prophet (as in John 1:21; 4:46; 7:40), the explicit and extended building on the prediction of the prophet's coming in Deut. 18 as fulfilled in Jesus is unique to Acts. How the hearers of his message respond to him is determinative of their place – or their forfeiture of a place – in the people of God.

Two other titles of Jesus which are found in Acts are "the holy and righteous one". Used in conjunction in Peter's sermon in the temple (3:14–16), these two terms stand in contrast with someone who fits neither descriptive adjective: the murderer (Barabbas) whom the religious leaders have asked to have released in place of Jesus. In contrast to this rejection of the Holy One of God by the religious authorities of Israel, the apostles bear testimony to who he is and what healing powers are at work through him. Similarly, in Stephen's speech he reminds his hearers that their ancestors killed the prophets "who announced beforehand the coming of the Righteous One, whom you have now betrayed and murdered" (7:52–53). Thus their sin stands in sharpest contrast to his righteousness, and their rejection of his message is counter to the work of the Holy Spirit (7:51) and to the law which God had given them through his angels (7:53).

Similarly, Paul's sermon in Pisidian Antioch notes that the people of Jerusalem and their rulers did not recognize who Jesus was nor understand the prophetic utterances about him, even though they fulfilled those prophecies by their rejection of him and by their request that Pilate execute him (13:27–28). God's having raised him from the dead shows that what happened to him was in accord with the scriptures, specifically the promise, "You will not let your holy one see corruption" (13:35).[12] Instead of his having been a sinner, as he was regarded by the religious leaders, he is the one through whom forgiveness of sins is made available by God. In rejecting him they are taking their place with the scoffers and unbelievers of whom the prophet Habakkuk warned (13:41; cf. Hab. 1:5). It is in this sense that Jesus is pictured in Acts as holy and righteous.

The term "name of Jesus" – in variant forms – assumes a function of great importance throughout Acts. Nearly one fourth of all the New Testament occurrences of the Greek word, *onoma*, are in Acts. The connotations of the name of Jesus are at least four. The first is that the name of Jesus is the ground of identity for God's new people, public testimony to which is given through baptism. At the conclusion of his Pentecost sermon, Peter calls for his hearers to be baptized in the name of Jesus Christ (2:38). The invitation is extended to his Jewish hearers ("you and your children") but also to Gentiles ("all that are afar off"; 2:39). The first step in this wider outreach of the gospel takes place in Samaria, where those who respond in faith to the preaching of Philip "about the kingdom of God and the name of Jesus Christ" are baptized, including Simon Magus (8:12–13). When Peter first preaches to the Gentile military officer, Cornelius, those who believe and receive the outpouring of the Holy Spirit are baptized "in the name of Jesus Christ" (10:44–48). The disciples[13] whom Paul found at Corinth, who knew nothing of the Holy Spirit, first are baptized "in the name of the Lord Jesus", and through the imposition of Paul's hands, receive the Spirit as well (19:1–6). Following Paul's arrest in Jerusalem (21:37–40), when he gave an account of his conversion through the appearance of Jesus of Nazareth to him, he tells that he was instructed by Ananias of Damascus to be baptized and to "call on the name" of Jesus (22:12–16). The name of Jesus – eight times Acts refers to him as "Jesus of Nazareth" – rather than a formal christological title is the ground of identity for members of this new community.

This name as the ground of identity carries with it a serious and solemn responsibility, however: to link oneself with this name is to invite official opposition or even martyrdom. Paul himself had set out to destroy the movement by binding all who called on the name of Jesus (9:14), but ironically he was called of God to carry the name of the Lord Jesus "before Gentiles and kings and the sons of Israel" (9:15). This responsibility was to involve him to suffer for the sake of that name (9:16). Later when the apostolic council in Jerusalem confirms the mission to the Gentiles undertaken by Paul and his associates, it is noted that they have "risked their lives for the sake of our Lord Jesus Christ" (15:24–26). Referring to these experiences of public hostility, Paul refuses to be deterred from going to Jerusalem by the predictions of the suffering he will experience there (21:7–12). He declares that he is ready to suffer imprisonment or even death "for the name of the Lord Jesus" (21:13). The irony moves full circle when, in the course of his self-defense before King Agrippa in Caesarea Paul tells how the focus of his initial efforts to destroy the Christian movement had been his opposition "to the name of Jesus of Nazareth" (26:9). He recalls this hostility toward Christianity just as he is about to be sent under arrest to plead his case for the non-political aims of the Jesus movement in Rome, the symbolic and actual center of the Gentile world empire. The issue from beginning to end is the "name of Jesus" as it is acclaimed and powerfully operative in the new community of faith.

Acts also describes Jesus as *archegos*, a term found only in this book and in the Letter to the Hebrews. In Greek literature, this designation is given to the founder of a city, to the originator of a movement, or to the political figure in charge of a state or city. In the more philosophical language of Hebrews, Jesus is the prototype of the one who achieves perfection through suffering (2:10). In Heb. 12:2 he is seen as the one who started the pattern of faithful obedience to God in the face of suffering and death and who has brought that mode of life to perfection. In a similar sense, Acts 3:15 reports Peter to have acclaimed Jesus as the model and agent of life, whose triumph over death was accomplished by God's action in raising him from the dead. The author of Acts then makes the point that this is not merely a nice theory: Peter and the other apostles are witnesses to what God has already done and continues to do through Jesus. In his response to the high priest's injunction against teaching in the name of Jesus (Acts 5:28) Peter asserts that what is at stake here is not a random choice or a frivolous decision to honor the crucified Jesus by assigning to him this grand title. Rather, it is God who has exalted Jesus as prototype (*archegos*) and savior and he is the ground for God's offer to Israel of repentance and the forgiveness of sins. To make the case even more emphatically, Peter declares that this is not simply a theological theory: the apostles form the core of those who have witnessed and who continue to witness to the truth claims being made. Furthermore, it is the Holy Spirit who enforces these claims "to those who obey him" (5:30–32). Jesus is far more than an outstanding example of faithful endurance and divine vindication. He is also the model for the new people that is being called into being through the testimony of the apostles, as the author of Acts attests throughout his writing.

4. Present and Future Roles of Jesus

As we have seen, Acts depicts Jesus in his present role as Son of God and Lord exalted at the right hand of God (2:33), from which position of honor he has poured out the Holy Spirit on the new community. It is from this exalted status that Jesus extends the offer of repentance to his people (5:31). Details of the glory of Jesus in the presence of God are added in the report of Stephen's vision of God and Christ at the conclusion of his speech (7:55–56). In his address in the temple portico (3:21) Peter observes that Jesus must remain in this glorious position until God has accomplished all that he promised through the prophets for the renewal of his people and of the whole of creation (3:19). Jesus' future role is to be that of "judge of the living and the dead" (10:42). But he is to be not only the future judge but also the present model for humanity by which all will be evaluated on that day that God has fixed, as Paul declares in his address to the Areopagites in Athens (17:31). The certainty of positive outcome of this divine assessment has already been provided for believers in God's having raised Jesus from the dead. This event has the potential to provide assurance to all humanity, although there will be those who will follow the example of the Areopagites by mocking this claim made for Jesus. As the archetype of obedience to the will and purpose of God, he is now the model for God's new people, and in the future he will be the criterion of judgment on all humanity.

3

The Spirit as God's Instrument in the Present Age

As noted at the end of the previous chapter, it is the exalted Lord Jesus who poured out the Holy Spirit, according to Acts 2:33. The connections and continuity between what God has done through Jesus and what he continues to do in the present age are through the Spirit and this claim is central to the theology of Acts. The links are already evident as early as Luke's account of the birth of Jesus. They continue in his record of the activity of Jesus in his gospel, as well as throughout the book of Acts.

1. The Role of the Spirit in the Life of Jesus

The frequency of references to the Spirit is greater in Acts than in all the gospels added together.[1] This is the more remarkable in view of the important role of the Spirit in Luke's gospel, where the infancy narratives report that Mary's child is to be born through the Holy Spirit (1:35), and the blessings of Mary and the child Jesus by Elizabeth and Simeon (1:41; 2:25–27) as well as Zechariah's praise to God for the birth of John the Baptist are all the result of insights provided through the Holy Spirit. Luke alone gives special emphasis to the role of the Spirit in the career of Jesus in his report that when the Spirit came upon Jesus at his baptism it took *bodily* form (3:22).[2] Thus for Luke the Spirit has a paramount function in setting the stage for the coming of Jesus and in his preparation for fulfilling his mission.

Most significant, however, is Luke's expansion of the Markan story of Jesus' rejection in the synagogue at Nazareth (Mark 6:1–6). Luke alone among the gospels includes an extended quotation from Isa. 61:1–2 about God's outpouring of his Spirit upon the "anointed" agent of his purpose, which promise Jesus then declares to have been "fulfilled in your hearing" (Luke 4:16–21). Although the title Christ/Messiah is not explicitly applied to Jesus in this Lukan account, the cognate verb (*echrisen*) is employed, and the import is that Jesus has been commissioned and divinely enabled to carry out this unique role, foretold by the prophets and now in process of fulfilment. Each detail of the Isaianic prophecy is relevant to the role of Jesus and of his commissioned followers in Acts: preaching the good news to the deprived and to those who by Jewish modes of covenantal definition were outsiders. Those to whom release is granted are those dominated by demonic powers; the blind are enabled to see;[3] the time for the inbreaking of God's rule is proclaimed. The enabling power by which this ministry of Jesus is portrayed by Luke as being carried forward is the Spirit of God which has come upon Jesus.

It is in harmony with these themes from the Gospel of Luke that in Acts 10 (Peter's sermon in the house of Cornelius), the career of Jesus is depicted as the outcome of God's having "anointed Jesus of Nazareth with power; how he went about doing good and healing all that were oppressed of the devil, for God was with him" (10:38). In the subsequent description of the career of Jesus in this passage, God is the one who raised Jesus from the dead, chose the apostolic witnesses, and charged them to testify that Jesus was ordained by God to be the judge of the living and the dead (10:40–42). The empowerment of Jesus and his messengers comes ultimately from God, but it is the Spirit of God which is the agent through whom God commissioned and enabled Jesus to fulfil his divinely ordained role. The Spirit is also represented in Acts as having a role in preparing the events and the actors through which God's purpose is achieved. Even though human agents seem to be opposing the purpose of God and his chosen agent, they are unwittingly instruments through whom that purpose is being fulfilled.

It is with this conviction of the divine control of history that Acts tells us also how, long before Jesus appeared on the scene, it was the Spirit who led David to foresee the coalition of Jewish and Gentile leaders who would try to destroy Jesus (Acts 4:25–28; cf. Ps. 2:1–2), just as the Spirit enabled Isaiah to foretell the rejection of Jesus (Acts 28:25–27; cf. Isa. 6:9–10). Likewise, the Spirit spoke through David concerning the one who was to betray Jesus (Acts 1:15–20; cf. Ps. 69:25; 109:8). As the author's reading of scripture attests in detail, these insights and advance knowledge of what God has planned for the redemption of his people through Jesus are granted through the Spirit.

2. The Spirit as the Instrument for Launching the Good News to the Ends of the Earth

The world-wide proclamation of the gospel is seen in Acts not as a novelty introduced by the apostles after the death and resurrection of Jesus, but as the fulfilment of the program announced to his disciples by the risen Lord. Indeed, it was already launched in principle through the activities of Jesus reported in the Lukan stories of his having extended healing and forgiveness beyond Israel to be carried out. This humanity-encompassing program is to be carried out through the power which the Holy Spirit will grant to them (Acts 1:8). That outpouring of the Spirit upon them to enable them to accomplish this task is said to have been predicted by Jesus during the time of his earlier associations with his followers (1:5), even though the account in the gospels attributes to John the Baptist this foretelling of the baptism with the Holy Spirit.[4]

The inaugural stage in the fulfilment of this divine promise is described as taking place on the day of Pentecost. The connotation which this festival day carried for Jews in the time of Jesus is important to be noted. In the Jewish apocryphal book of Jubilees, which dates from the mid-second century BCE, the Feast of Pentecost[5] has lost its original significance as a harvest festival and has become a celebration of the renewal of the covenant. After linking the feast with Noah (Jub. 7:34–37), Jubilees focusses primarily on Abraham (Jub. 15:1–16; 22:1–9), who prays for a son whose posterity "might become an elect people . . . and an inheritance for all the nations of the earth from henceforth and for all the days of the generations of the earth forever." In Jub. 14:1–6 Jacob is described as keeping this feast at Beersheba, whereupon he is given divine confirmation of this meaning of the feast when he experiences a theophany of the God of the covenant. It is with these connotations of covenant renewal and inclusiveness that Acts describes the outpouring of the Holy Spirit in Acts 2, adding to it the explicit and detailed claim of the fulfilment of Joel's prophecy (Joel 3:1–5). Covenant renewal is thus depicted in Acts as world-wide in scope and as potentially universal in its inclusiveness.

The sound of the rushing wind (*pnoe*) from heaven is an aural metaphor for the coming of the Spirit (*pneuma*) which filled the whole house where the apostles were gathered (2:1–2). A visual metaphor then occurs, in which "tongues as of fire [were seen] distributed and resting upon each one of them" (2:3). The import of the vision of tongues is immediately apparent when the apostles begin "to speak in other tongues, as the Spirit gave them utterance". The visual pun on "tongues" is obvious, but it is essential to note that, unlike the charismatic gift of tongues that Paul discusses in I Corinthians 12 and 14, there is in this event in Acts no need for an interpreter (in contrast to I Cor. 12:10; 14:1–19). Instead there is in this story in Acts a simultaneous miracle: the apostles are enabled to speak in languages other than their own, and the listeners from every part of the world hear the message in their own native languages. It is not surprising that the latter "were amazed and wondered" that they could understand these Galileans without an interpreter (2:7). What these festival visitors from all parts of Eurasia, Mesopotamia, Africa, Mediterranean lands and islands, and Arabia heard was a description of "the mighty works of God", recounted "in our own tongues" (2:7–11). Clearly, what is described as taking place is not merely a miraculous linguistic translation but comprehension across cultures of what God has done and continues to do on behalf of his covenant people.

Peter's address makes the direct claim: "This is what was spoken by the prophet Joel" (2:16). The event does not merely resemble what Joel predicted, nor does Joel merely provide a framework for understanding what is happening. For Peter, this is it! The passage quoted from Joel in 2:17–21 makes the point with great effectiveness that participation in the blessings which God is pouring out on the human race is open to all human beings ("all flesh"), regardless of age, sexual, or social distinctions. The comprehensiveness of the invitation to share

is made explicit in the final sentence quoted from Joel (2:21):
"And it shall be that *whoever* calls on the name of the Lord shall
be saved." The one significant shift from the words of Joel to
those of Peter in Acts is apparent in the final half of the sermon,
which culminates in the quotation from Ps. 110 and the
declaration that "God has made both *Lord* and Christ, this
Jesus whom you crucified" (2:36). To "call on the name of the
Lord" no longer means simply to invoke the name of Yahweh,
God of Israel. It now signifies the gaining of a new identity by
an act of public commitment to Jesus. As Peter declares,
"Repent, and be baptized every one of you in the name of
Jesus Christ for the forgiveness of your sins, and you shall
receive the gift of the Holy Spirit" (2:38).

Inseparably interrelated here are (1) the confession of, and
identification with the name of Jesus; (2) the public testimony
and identity claim through the rite of baptism, and (3) the
receiving of the Holy Spirit. To have received the Spirit in
Acts is the divine confirmation of renewal and covenantal
participation. According to Acts 2:41, the number of those who
received this word and were baptized reached the impressive
figure of three thousand on this day of covenant renewal.
From this point on the common life of the community has four
dimensions as here described: devotion to hearing the teaching
of the apostles; participation in the shared existence of the
community;[6] the breaking of bread (the eucharist); and the
common prayers. All this becomes effective for the new
covenant people through the outpouring of the Spirit.

Acts notes that among those present in the throngs of the
pious gathered in Jerusalem at Pentecost were "visitors from
Rome, both Jews and proselytes" (2:10). *Epidemountes*, which
is regularly translated "visitors", probably refers to expatriates:
that is, to Jews and proselytes from Rome who had taken up
residence in Jerusalem, but whose native tongue would have
been Latin. It is also possible that they were god-fearers, or
more accurately God-seekers, who had come to Jerusalem in
their effort to find and identify with the God of Israel, although
if they were not formally proselytes, they would not have been
part of the Jewish community, which would have run counter
to the phases of outreach beyond Judaism which Acts so
carefully details in chapters 7 and 8. In either case these former
residents of Rome are symbolic representatives, not only of
non-Palestinian Jews who in the middle decades of the first

century were soon to join the Christian community throughout the Roman world, but also of the natives of Rome, the city where Paul will be bearing witness to Christ by the time the book of Acts ends. Probably a significant portion of these "visitors" were not birth-right Jews, but had been attracted to consider participation in the covenant people of Israel, presumably at the adult level and surely by personal choice. It is upon such geographically and culturally diverse human beings that the Spirit has been poured out from the outset in the Acts narrative. The Spirit will confirm the witness of the apostles, since God has granted this Spirit "to those who obey him" (5:32), whoever they may be.

The first direct step in the apostles' reaching out beyond birth-right Jews and proselyte converts is described in Acts 6. The development comes as a consequence of the tensions between the semitic-speaking (Hebrews) and the Greek-speaking (hellenist) Jews within the earliest Christian community. The immediate problem was discrimination against non-semitic-speaking members of the community in the distribution of food and funds.[7] The choice of Greek-speaking leaders for dealing with this problem was based on the candidates being "of good repute, full of the Spirit and of wisdom" (6:1–3). Stephen, as one of this group, is characterized as "a male who is full of faith and of the Holy Spirit" (6:5). In his extended address (Acts 7) he denounces those who cannot accept his dismissal of the temple and its cultus as unnecessary to the rapprochement of humans with God, and in so doing he declares that these who insist on preserving unchanged the assumptions from the past about where God is and how his people can come to know him "always resist the Holy Spirit" (7:51). Stephen's experience at the moment when he faces a martyr's death is roughly analogous to that of Jesus, when the certainty of his own death became apparent, and he was granted a vision of God in the transfiguration (Mark 9:2–8). Now, in the moment that he faces death in fulfilling the role to which God has called him, the Spirit enables him to see the enthroned Christ at God's right hand (7:55). In this way the divine approval of Stephen's message of a non-localized and non-ethnic-oriented approach to God is confirmed by the Spirit in the Acts account.

Philip began preaching the gospel of Christ to those who were geographically and religiously closest to the Jews: the

Samaritans (8:5). The apostolic approval of this new stage in the enlargement of the new community beyond the limits of Judaism is given through Peter and John who, on visiting the Samaritan believers, prayed for them and laid hands on them so that they might receive the Holy Spirit (8:16–17). The result is that indeed "they received the Holy Spirit". The attempt of Simon the magician to purchase the power to bestow the Spirit by the laying on of hands is rejected, but his request heightens the sense of the dramatic and potent force which the Spirit is seen to convey (8:18–24). Similarly, it is the Spirit that prepares Philip for his next venture in extending the gospel beyond the pale of Judaism, when the Spirit urges him to join the Ethiopian eunuch as he is returning from his pious journey to Jerusalem unable to understand the words of the prophet about the one who dies like a slaughtered sheep and whose life is taken up from the earth (8:27–34). Philip's christological interpretation of the text of Isa. 53:7–8 is effective, and confirmation of Philip's mission is given through the Spirit which transports him to Ashdod (8:39–40).

Each successive stage of the outreach of the gospel to the wider world receives confirmation by the Spirit. Thus, the conversion of Saul/Paul from chief threat to major apostle is given when Ananias conveys the message to Paul from the risen Christ who had appeared to him in his vision, promising him restoration of sight and *the gift of the Spirit* (9:17). Peter likewise was prepared by the Spirit for his role as the first to bear witness to Christ among Gentiles, represented here by the Roman military officer, Cornelius (Acts 10). That this was not merely a private experience of Peter but a major step in the expansion of the community is indicated when the Spirit – this time without any laying on of hands by the apostles – comes down in sovereign fashion on all who heard Peter's sermon. Understandably, the pious Jews who had accompanied Peter on this launching of the mission to Gentiles "were amazed because the gift of the Spirit had been poured out even on Gentiles" (10:45). Once the gift of the Spirit has been bestowed, the community gives public confirmation of its members' participation in the common life of the group through the rite of baptism (10:47–48). This basic issue is aired in the apostolic circle in Jerusalem by those who insist that all members of the covenant people must first be circumcised. In response, Peter recounts his experience in the initial proclamation of the gospel to Gentile hearers, including the vision, the guidance by the Spirit (11:12), and the confirmatory outpouring of the Spirit on the Gentile believers (11:15–16). This latter crucial detail is repeated at the apostolic council described in Acts 15, where the gift of the Spirit to the Gentile believers is seen as God's own witness to the propriety and importance of this development which has redefined the ground for sharing in God's new people (15:8).

The next stage in the spread of the gospel occurs when those driven out of the Judaean Christian community during the crisis that arose with the Hellenists' preaching to Gentiles are effective in the conversion of Gentiles in Phoenicia, Antioch, Cyprus and Cyrene (11:19–20). The gospel is taking root in, and nuclei of the Christian community are alive in the islands and coast of the eastern Mediterranean from Africa to northern Syria. The one chosen to investigate and evaluate this development, Barnabas, is described as "a good man, full of the Holy Spirit and of faith" (11:24). In this context another innovation occurs: the members of the community in Antioch "were for the first time called Christians" (11:26). Community definition is in process.

The crucial decision reached by the church in Antioch to commission Barnabas and Saul specifically to carry out a mission of the gospel in Gentile regions is depicted as taking place in the worshipping community there on instruction from the Holy Spirit (13:1–2). The Spirit enables Paul to make the proper decisions and to exercise authority as he undertakes this new phase of the life of the covenant people (13:9).

3. The Spirit as Agent of Confirmation of Community Membership

We have seen that the rite of baptism is linked throughout Acts with the initiatory or confirmatory activity of the Spirit, and that the movement of Peter and the other apostles is guided by the Spirit. In contrast to the spontaneity of these activities of the Spirit, however, in Acts 15 there is an institutional decision that is reached by the apostles assembled in Jerusalem. The issue had arisen at the impetus of members of the community who were of Pharisaic background, who insisted that circumcision and conformity to the law of Moses were requisite for all believers (15:5). This position was taken

by them in spite of the report of the success of the mission by
Paul and Barnabas to the Gentiles and of the flourishing of the
communities in Phoenicia and Samaria (15:3–4). In the solemn
assembly of the apostles in Jerusalem, Peter reminds them of
the Spirit's having fostered and sanctioned his mission to the
Gentiles (15:7–8), and enunciates the principles that God
makes no distinction between Jews and Gentiles: both kinds
of people experience cleansing of the heart by faith, rather
than by conformity to legal requirements. It is God's grace in
Jesus, not obedience to the precepts of the law through which
God saves his people (15:10–11). The effectiveness of Paul and
Barnabas in their work among the Gentiles has been confirmed
by signs and wonders accomplished among them, but James
points out that it is also in keeping with the words of the
prophets that the opportunity has been opened whereby "the
rest of humanity may seek the Lord" with the result that
Gentiles will be called by God's name (15:12–18; Amos 9:11–12;
Jer. 12:15; Isa. 45:21). Accordingly he articulates the basic
principle that only a minimum of requirements from the Law
of Moses are to be binding on Gentile believers.[8] The role
of the Spirit in this corporate decision-making process is
articulated by James, who declares that this policy "seemed
good to the Holy Spirit and to us" (15:28). Throughout Acts it
is the Spirit that is seen as the primary agent at work in the
early Christian communities to guide and shape policy on the
issue of admission to the new covenant people.

4. The Spirit as the Agent of Empowerment and Guidance

In the opening lines of Acts we read that, before Jesus was
taken up to God, he gave "commandment through the Holy
Spirit to the apostles whom he had chosen" (1:2). They are to
remain in Jerusalem until "the promise of the Father" is
fulfilled through the outpouring of the Spirit upon them to
enable them to carry out the task to which they have been
called (1:4–5). The power which will come upon them through
the Spirit will enable them to "be my witnesses in Jerusalem
and in all Judaea and Samaria, and to the end of the earth"
(1:8). When the Spirit comes upon them and fills them, the
apostles are enabled to launch their work, which will eventu-
ally encompass the whole earth (2:1–4). That the source of
the power by which the apostles are able to carry out their

astounding work of communication of the gospel and healing
is a paramount question is voiced by the high priestly group
when they interrogate the apostles (4:1–7). Peter, the spokesman for the group, is said to be filled with the Spirit when
he declares that it is through "the name of Jesus Christ of
Nazareth" that the healing of the lame man in the temple
occurred (4:8–10). Confirmation of the understanding of the
apostles as to the significance they perceive in Jesus, the
crucified, exalted Lord and the healings and wonders that are
taking place through his name is granted by God when,
following their prayer, "the place in which they were gathered
was shaken, and they were all filled with the Holy Spirit and
spoke the word of God with boldness" (4:27–31). Acts in this
way underscores the central role of the Spirit in directing and
enabling the apostles to carry out their work. The concrete
results, in the form of healings and such discernible actions
as the shaking of the place where they were assembled,
demonstrate to them the continuing presence and power of
the Spirit among them.

It is the Spirit that enables the Christian leadership to foresee
and make preparations for difficulties that lie ahead in the
future. A prophet from Jerusalem named Agabus "foretold by
the Holy Spirit" (11:28) that during a famine that would spread
across the world in the reign of the emperor Claudius (41–54
CE) it would be essential for believers in places like Antioch to
send money for the support of the Jerusalem-based elders.
Such funds were sent there through Barnabas and Saul (11:30).
Not only the spread of the gospel but the sustenance of its
central leaders benefit from the work of the Holy Spirit in their
midst.

In Acts the Spirit also serves as an instrument for limitation
of activity or warning of suffering for those at work in the
proclamation of the gospel. After his break with Barnabas and
his return to Syria and Cilicia, Paul chose Timothy to be his
companion and co-worker in evangelism and in "strengthen-
ing the churches" (15:36–16:5). As the two set out across the
provinces of Phrygia and Galatia (in the central part of Asia
Minor), they were "forbidden by the Holy Spirit" to speak the
message of Christ in Asia and "the Spirit of Jesus" would not
allow them to enter the province of Bithynia (16:6–7). The
eastern and southern regions were open to them, as they had
been in the past, and also the districts along the Aegean coast

opposite Macedonia (16:8). No explanation is offered in Acts for this limitation of the scope of their apostolic witness, but it is possible that a historical clue to what lies behind this enigmatic pronouncement is to be found in the First Letter of Peter. There we read that those addressed are residents of various provinces in Asia Minor, including Asia and Bithynia (I Peter 1:1). It seems likely that these territories had been evangelized by Peter or by others associated with him. In order to avoid any feeling of competition among the apostles or of conflict between points of view represented respectively by the Petrine and Pauline wings of the early church, the Spirit (in the Acts account) simply forbids Paul and his associates to carry on evangelistic or church-strengthening activities in those regions.

Also indicated in Acts are the ways in which the Spirit directs the itinerary of Paul, while at the same time making him aware of the personal difficulties which he must endure in the discharge of his ministry. Both the immediate and the longer range goals of Paul are disclosed when he resolves "in the Spirit" to return from Corinth by way of Macedonia and Achaia on his way to Jerusalem. Beyond these immediate destinations lies his expectation of journeying to Rome (19:21). En route to Jerusalem, Paul has a visit with the elders of the church at Ephesus (20:17). He reminds them of his service to the Lord and of what he had suffered as a result of plots against him (20:19). This had not deterred him from proclaiming his message of Christ in public to Jews and Greeks alike and instructing the Christians in private houses (20:21). Now, however, he knows himself to be "bound in the Spirit" to accept the "imprisonments and afflictions" that he is soon to experience "in every city", but especially in Jerusalem (20:22–23). He knows this because this is what the Holy Spirit has testified to him. On landing in Syria, Paul was told by certain members of the Christian community there "through the Spirit" that he ought not to go to Jerusalem (21:4).

Similarly, on reaching Caesarea, a seaport on the upper Palestinian coast, Paul is warned by the word and symbolic act of a Christian prophet, named Agabus, of the consequences of his going to Jerusalem. Agabus bound his hands and feet with Paul's girdle, declaring that the Holy Spirit has told him that this will be Paul's experience at the hand of the Jewish authorities in Jerusalem and that he will be turned over to the

Gentile officials there. In spite of this prophetic warning through the Spirit, which was followed by pleading from members of the local Christian community, Paul is persuaded and resolved to make the journey. He knows full well what the consequences may be, including the possibility of his martyrdom in Jerusalem "for the name of the Lord Jesus" (21:13). Those concerned about his welfare yield to his conviction, in spite of the warning by the Spirit, and conclude simply, "The will of the Lord be done" (21:14). The Spirit is the agent of warning, of restriction, but above all, of prophetic information as to the solemn consequences – which may be tragic, humanly speaking – of the life devoted to God's work in the world for the calling together of his new people.

5. The Spirit as Instrument of Judgment

Although Stephen denounces the Jewish leaders as "stiff-necked people, uncircumcized in heart and ears" because they "always resist the Holy Spirit" (7:51), he does not go on to indicate what the consequences of this resistance to the Spirit are. Elsewhere in Acts, however, the intention to exploit the power of the Spirit has dire consequences. When Ananias and Sapphira withhold part of the funds from the sale of a property, their deceit is described as having allowed Satan to fill their heart by lying to the Holy Spirit (5:3). On hearing this accusation, Ananias fell down dead (5:5). Later his wife continues the deceit, which Peter describes as an agreement together "to tempt the Spirit of the Lord", and she too is struck dead (5:7–10).

Two other stories of the dire consequences of exploitation of, or resistance to the Holy Spirit are told in Acts. In Samaria among the converts to Christianity was Simon, a practitioner of magic, who had attracted a large group of supporters and was acclaimed by them as "that power of God which is called Great" (8:9–11). Simon joined the men and women who had been his admirers, and shared with them astonishment at the marvellous acts that were performed through the apostle Philip (8:12–13). So impressed was Simon by the transformations that came as the consequence of the outpouring of the Holy Spirit through the apostles who visited Samaria that he offered to pay what was necessary so that he could lay hands on people and bestow the Spirit on them (8:18–19). Peter denounces his offer and warns him of possibly fatal consequences because his "heart is not right with God" and he is "in the gall of bitterness and the bond of iniquity" (8:21–23). A ray of hope remains for him if he repents and is forgiven, which leads Simon to ask Peter to pray for him (8:24).

The second of these stories of divine judgment through the Spirit is told in 13:7–12, where Elymas, who is described as "a Jewish false prophet" tries to dissuade the proconsul on the island of Cyprus from giving heed to the gospel as proclaimed by Paul and Barnabas. Filled with the Holy Spirit, Paul denounces him as a son of the devil, the enemy of all righteousness, as full of deceit and villainy, as perverter of the paths of the Lord, upon which he is struck blind. The proconsul is understandably impressed by this imprecation and its consequences for Elymas. The active agent in this narrative is the Spirit.

Paralleling both the Spirit's acts of deliverance of the apostles and works of judgment in the Acts narratives are the activities of the angels. When the apostles are imprisoned by the authorities in Jerusalem prior to their initial hearing before the council, an angel of the Lord is said to have opened the prison doors, allowing them to escape and instructing them to go bear public testimony in the temple to "the words of life" (5:19–20). It is an angel that tells Philip to go out on the road from Jerusalem to Gaza (8:26), though without giving him advance information concerning what he will experience there. It is an angel who appears to Cornelius, the Roman military officer, telling him to expect a visit from Peter (10:3–7). This is reported by the messengers who come to Peter to invite him to visit Cornelius (10:22). The importance of these details about how God has been preparing for the conversion of this Gentile is underscored when they are repeated in Peter's account of the event before the apostles in Jerusalem (11:13).

Imprisoned by Herod Agrippa, Peter was visited in his cell by angel who caused his chains to drop off and instructed him to leave the prison. He passed the guards unchallenged and the iron gate of the city opened before him before the angel left him (12:1–10). The Christians gathered at the house of John Mark are astounded when their prayer for Peter's deliverance is thus answered. Similarly, Paul is given reassurance by an angel that the storm-tossed ship on which he is being transported to Rome will reach a safe destination, and that he will one day stand before the emperor in Rome (27:21–25). Yet another mode of communication of God's purpose according to Acts is the vision. Two important examples of this are found in 16:9, where Paul at Troas has a nocturnal vision of a man from Macedonia, pleading with him to cross the Aegean Sea and offer help to the Macedonians. He knows instantly that this is the call of God, and makes plans to undertake the journey into this new land in order to preach the gospel there on the continent of Europe (16:10). Faced with the challenge of carrying on his work in Corinth after the majority of the Jews there had rejected him and his message, Paul is given reassurance about his mission to the Gentiles through a vision in which the Lord tells him to be unafraid, that he is safe from attack, and that there are many of his new people in this great pagan city (18:9–10). Thus, although the agents of divine disclosure differ in the Acts accounts – Spirit, angels, visions – it is through these extraordinary modes of communication that the purpose of God is known and the encouragement offered to the apostles to carry forward their work.

The angels as instruments of divine punishment appear in Acts as well. When Herod Agrippa, decked in splendid robes and declaiming an oration from the throne, allows the people to acclaim him as not human but a god, he is struck down by an angel of the Lord, is eaten by worms and dies (12:20–23). The author of Acts is consistent in showing the means by which God is at work in the world for human transformation and renewal, or for the destruction of those who oppose or pervert his purposes.

4

Reaching out across Religious and Cultural Boundaries

1. Beginning in Jerusalem

The vivid account in Acts 2 of the outpouring of the Spirit on the day of Pentecost, with a cast drawn from all parts of the civilized world of the first century, involves far more than the prospect of merely geographical extension of the people of God. What is anticipated by the author of Acts in this symbolic scene is the reconstitution of the covenant people in such a way as to bridge over ethnic, cultic, social, cultural and religious distinctions. What is to happen, as we have noted, is not the replacement of the old by the new, but a process of transformation which builds on the heritage of Israel's past toward the creation of a new and inclusive community that is nevertheless in continuity with essential features of the traditional factors of covenantal definition. It is essential in portraying this development, therefore, that the starting point be Jerusalem.

The risen Christ gives the disciples the order that they are "not to depart from Jerusalem" (Acts 1:4). It is there that God is believed to dwell in the innermost court of the temple, and it is there that Jews from all over the world come to approach their God, to offer sacrifices, and to receive forgiveness and reconciliation. It is in this city that the religious leaders of Judaism are concentrated, including the priests, the scribes whose task it is to interpret and show the relevance of the law of Moses, as well as the religious parties of the Pharisees and the Sadducees. It is there that, in accord with Roman policy for administering ethnic territories which it controls, the leading citizens meet as a council to determine regional social and religious policies (4:5). It was in the temple courts there that throngs of local and visiting Jews gathered, as well as pious or curious non-Jews, who were permitted to enter the Court of the Gentiles. It is in Solomon's Portico within the temple compound that the angel of the Lord instructs the apostles to go and preach to the crowds (5:12, 20). All those addressed are physically and functionally within the structure of Judaism as it existed in the first century CE.

The issue as to the significance of Jesus for the future of the covenant people comes to a head dramatically when the apostles are brought before the council (5:27–42). In spite of the council's injunction prohibiting the apostles from teaching in the name of Jesus, they have "filled Jerusalem" with their teaching and placed the blame for his death on the council. Their response is that God has raised from the dead and exalted to his right hand the one killed by action of the council. God has done this "to give repentance to Israel and forgiveness of sins". As a counter to the rage which these charges and claims evoke from the members of the council, one of the members – Gamaliel, a Pharisee – reminds them of failed recent Jewish insurrectionist movements, offering the advice that the Jesus movement will fail as well if it is not of God. Then he adds, "But if it is of God, you will not be able to overthrow them. You might even be found opposing God" (5:39). The result is that, except for some corporal punishment, the apostles are free to continue to bear testimony and offer instruction in the temple concerning Jesus as the Messiah (5:42). Jerusalem and its temple, therefore, serve as the launching platform for the movement that will soon reach across the Roman world, not just geographically but socially and culturally.

The first stage in this socio-cultural outreach is described briefly and somewhat enigmatically in Acts 6:1–6. As the membership in the movement increased, there was a division along cultural and linguistic lines between the Hebrews and the Hellenists. It is essential to bear in mind that there was no uniform position among first-century Jews of Palestine on such a basic issue as the ground of participation in the covenant people. Nor was there an official stance among the Jewish leaders as to the proper attitude of Jews toward Gentiles and Gentile culture. It is remarkable that the oldest buildings in Galilee identified by archaeologists as synagogues (which date from the third and fourth centuries CE) have Greek inscriptions and regularly include as a central feature the signs of the zodiac on their mosaic floors and Yahweh represented as Helios, driving the chariot of the sun.[1] There is mounting evidence that Jews in Galilee in the first and second centuries CE were bilingual.[2] Mere linguistic preference would not have been an issue among Jews or Palestinian Christians. The fact that all seven of the Hellenists who are chosen have Greek names (6:5) is another indication that the dynamic operative in this controversy is not simply linguistic, but cultural as well. The occasion for the dispute is said to be inequality in the distribution of supplies to members of the community – a practice which is discussed below in Chapter 5. But as we shall see, the group associated with Stephen later comes under attack because its members invite Gentiles to take part in the new community (11:19–21). It is significant from the sociological perspective that those who take the initiative in trying to get rid of Stephen and the movement that he represents are themselves Jews from various parts of the Diaspora and hence under the influence of Graeco-Roman culture (6:9). People with such a background would be especially sensitive to the issues which arise among those who are seeking to maintain identity with a tradition from a non-western culture and to do so in the midst of the culturally aggressive world of the Roman empire, with its pressures for social and religious conformity. It is Jews who in the diaspora have wrestled with these cross-cultural issues, who take the initiative in bringing charges against Stephen and his associates that what they are proposing is the dismantling of the temple and the law: the factors which are central to Jewish religious identity (6:9–14). The issue is succinctly articulated in the accusation that these Hellenists "will change the customs which Moses delivered to us". This threatens the ground-rules for covenantal participation.

It is to this issue, rather than to discrimination in welfare distribution, that Stephen devotes his speech (Acts 7). The subtle but cumulatively powerful thrust of his address is that God is not and never has been localized as the ground of his relationship to his people. When God first appeared to Abraham in order to establish the basis for the covenant relationship, it was when the patriarch was living in Mesopotamia (7:2). Even when he came to the land of Palestine, God gave him no claim to any part of it, "not even a foot's length", but promised that it would be part of the inheritance of his posterity (7:4–5). The point of God's action was that even Abraham's descendants would be "aliens in a land belonging to others", where they would be enslaved and ill-treated. It was in Egypt that Joseph and his father Jacob received the promises of deliverance from bondage, and Jacob returned to the land of Palestine only as a corpse (7:9–16).

The same factors are evident in Stephen's account of Moses, who "was instructed in all the wisdom of the Egyptians". Moses was rejected and threatened by his fellow Israelites, and had to take refuge in the land of the Midianites. It was in the land of Sinai that God appeared to Moses, and it was in Egypt and by the Red Sea that God manifested his power, but the people of Israel rejected his leadership and preferred to remain in Egypt, offering sacrifices to idols (7:30–41), as the prophet Amos later reminded them (Amos 5:25–27 = Acts 7:42–43). The people were warned in advance that their failure to honor God properly would result in their exile in Babylon (7:43). Throughout their early history, the tabernacle as the locus of God's presence among his people was mobile in the wilderness and in the land, until it was brought into the land under Joshua. Later, David decided to give it a permanent location and Solomon actually erected the temple as God's house (7:45–48). At that point Stephen quotes from Second Isaiah the declarations and rhetorical questions which challenge the very notion that God's dwelling can be localized – even in the splendid temple in Jerusalem (Isa. 66:1–2 = Acts 7:49–50). The gross misunderstanding of relationship with God that the temple embodies is matched by the consistent rejection of God's messengers, the prophets, by the leaders of the Jews. Indeed, they have failed to keep the law, even though God gave it to them through the angels (7:51–53). The argument, therefore, is not over the law but concerns the human institution – the temple – through which the law is institutionalized and in terms of which its requirements are understood. The potentially universal reign and presence of God are affirmed in the quotation from Second Isaiah, and Stephen's colleagues, who live and work after his martyrdom, will seek to make that message and invitation available across ethnic and social barriers.

The conclusions to be drawn from the address of Stephen are radical in terms of temple-oriented Judaism concerned primarily to preserve Palestinian land and culture. The worship of God had been localized in Jerusalem at the temple only temporarily. God had appeared to the patriarchs in various lands, with the covenant first broached to Abraham in Mesopotamia and the law given to Moses in Sinai. The prophet had announced that no one could build a residence for God, but the present leaders insist on making it the central and exclusive ground of relationship to God. Their characteristic rejection of the prophetic messengers that God has sent them over the centuries is now matched by their rejection of Jesus.

The death of Stephen and the persecution of the church in Jerusalem do not bring a halt to the revolutionary views and program of the Hellenists, however. Instead of their activities being concentrated in Jerusalem, they are "scattered through-out the region of Judaea and Samaria" (8:1). Samaria was something other than another geographical district of Palestine in which Jews lived. Samaria included Shechem, where the tribes of Israel entered into a covenant with each other and with God after they came into the land following the Exodus from Egypt and where the basic laws and regulations for their common life were laid down (Josh. 24). The place was associated with Abraham (Gen. 12:6) and Jacob (Gen. 34), and was the place where the latter's body was laid to rest (Josh. 23:32). The deity honored there was the God of the Covenant (Judges 9:46). It was there that all Israel came to make Reho-boam their King (I Kings 12:1), and the city was rebuilt when the northern tribes established their own royal line (I Kings 12:25). Omri, who established the northern kingdom of Israel on a firm basis, built a new capital city at Samaria on a hill that dominated major trade routes north and south, east and west (I Kings 16:21–24). The central shrine for Israel was at Bethel to the south of Samaria. When the Assyrian armies invaded Israel in 722 BCE, the cities of Shechem and Samaria were destroyed. In the fifth century, the Persians separated the land into two districts: Samaria to the north and Judaea to the south. The Samaritans tried to thwart the redevelopment of Judaea and Jerusalem, with the result that a strong antipathy developed between the two districts. By the fourth century BCE, an abortive revolt by the Samaritans against their hellenistic rulers led to their expulsion from the city. Shifting their base back to Shechem, they built a new shrine to their deity on Mount Gerizim, overlooking the valley east of Samaria. The new city, Neapolis,[3] grew up at the foot of the mountain and continues to the present day to be the center for the worship of God by the Samaritans and their priests. According to Josephus, the Samaritans were not of Israelite origins but were brought to the land from Persia. Convinced that their god had failed them, they asked the king of Assyria to assign to them some of the priests of Israel who might teach them about a new deity,[4] the God of Israel. Whatever the origins of the group may have been, by the first century they had competing claims to be the true heirs of the covenant, competing versions of the Pentateuch, and competing shrines where God was said to be in their midst. The official Jewish attitude toward the Samaritans was that they were perverters of the worship of God and of the law of God, so that they were to be denounced and contact with them avoided.

In sharp contrast, the members of the church who had been driven out of Jerusalem to escape persecution there now are addressing their message to the Samaritans, despised as they are as violators of the covenant. In sharp contrast, these messengers of Christ invite the Samaritans to share in the redefined covenant people. The effectiveness and appropriateness of this preaching of the gospel to them is demonstrated by the signs which are performed among them: exorcisms and healings (8:4–7). Peter and John travel to Samaria to survey what is reported to have taken place through the Christian witness there, and the confirmation comes through the outpouring of the Holy Spirit. Peter and John add their own approval to this new undertaking by "preaching the gospel to many villages of the Samaritans" (8:25).

A similar development in a different direction, geographically and ethnically, is depicted in 8:26–40. The Ethiopian eunuch is an official in the royal establishment of Ethiopia. Eunuchs were valued in ancient monarchic establishments because they were not subject to corruption through sexual enticement and could even preside over such sensitive operations as royal harems. They were prohibited in Mosaic law, however, from so much as entering the assembly of God's people (Deut. 23:1). In the vivid scene of the eunuch reading aloud from the scroll of Isaiah as he rolls along in his chariot, we have an image of an earnest seeker after the God of Israel. His inability to understand the import of what he is reading is symbolic of the condition of Gentile seekers. Although Acts gives no details of Philip's exegesis of Isa. 53, the text serves as the point of departure for Philip's proclamation of the gospel. The eunuch knows that for him to become a member of the new community he must be baptized, and he is, there being a convenient source of supply along the Gaza road. Philip's return route takes him through Ashdod and the predominantly hellenized cities of the sea coast as far north as Caesarea. The pattern of inclusion of non-Jews as hearers of the gospel and therefore as potential participants in the new covenant is being considerably extended.

In the midst of these accounts of the gospel crossing over ethnic and cultural boundaries, Acts describes the most vivid and radical shift of all: the conversion of Paul. Unlike the evidence from his letters, which show how deeply Paul was influenced by hellenistic culture, especially Stoic philosophy, there are no details in Acts which portray Paul as other than a totally committed champion of the preservation of ethnic and cultic boundaries for the people of God. The various accounts of Paul's conversion throughout Acts provide additional details about Paul's commitments and strategies in his pre-conversion attempts to stamp out the Christian movement. His birth in the province of Cilicia on the border between Syria and Asia Minor – in what was presumably a hellenistic cultural environment – stands in contrast to the education he experienced in Jerusalem under Gamaliel, a strict interpreter of the Jewish law (22:3). Paul in his letters refers to Antioch as presumably his place of residence prior to his conversion, and makes no mention of Tarsus, the city in the province of Cilicia with which he is linked in Acts 9:11; 21:39. Perhaps the author of Acts knew that Tarsus was a major center of hellenistic learning. Strategically located with a fine seaport and at the terminus of the only road which led from Syria and the east across the Taurus mountain to central Asia Minor, Tarsus was given status as a free city in the mid-first century BCE, and under Augustus became the leading intellectual center of the eastern Mediterranean, eclipsing Athens and Alexandria. It was especially noted for the Stoic philosophers who taught there, including Zeno, the pioneer of Stoic philosophy. Paul uses Stoic terminology throughout his letters, and in his speech in Athens (Acts 17) he quotes the poet Aratus, who came from Cilicia and possibly from Tarsus. In his autobiographical sketch in Acts, however, he speaks exclusively of his training in the interpretation of the Jewish law. Central to his devotion to "the law of our fathers" was his program of stamping out the Jesus movement (which he refers to as "the Way"; 9:2; 22:4; 24:14) by carting off its adherents to the authorities in Jerusalem. His approval of the execution of Stephen, the violator of those legal norms, which is mentioned in passing in Acts 8:1, was fully consonant with this program of stamping out "the Way". His scheme of bringing before the Jewish authorities in Jerusalem any Christian believers, male or female, he might find in Damascus (9:1–3) is seen in Acts to have been motivated by his strict reading of the Jewish law. In 26:9–11 he adds further details concerning his program of opposition to Jesus and the movement that had arisen in his name, including placing "the saints" in prison, joining in the vote for their execution, punishing them in the synagogues, and persecuting them in foreign cities (26:9–11).

In Paul's own account of his conversion (Gal. 1:11–17) there is mention only of his violent efforts to destroy the church, and how following his vision of the Christ, he spent some time in Arabia and then returned to Damascus. There is no hint of cooperation with the priestly or scribal authorities before his conversion, and none of his conferring initially with the Christian leaders in Jerusalem after his experience of the risen Lord. Indeed, he adds the detail that he was unknown by sight to the churches of Christ in Judaea, although they heard of his persecuting activity – presumably in Damascus, or perhaps elsewhere in Syria as well (Gal. 1:18–23).[5] By concentrating the Pauline persecution of the church in Jerusalem, Acts heightens both the antipathy of the official Jewish leadership based there toward the Jesus movement, as well as the implication that it was there that the movement began, rather than in Galilee, as the gospel tradition indicates.[6] On one basic point the accounts of Paul's conversion in Acts and Galatians agree: the former persecutor of the church is now the primary witness to non-Israelites (Gal. 1:23; cf. Acts 9:15). Yet he continues to bear testimony to the Jews in Damascus that Jesus was the Christ (Acts 9:22). In the Acts narrative, Paul's situation is compounded with irony: the Jews, whose strict definition of covenantal participation he had sought to uphold (9:21) now plot to kill him (9:23). Similarly, when in Acts he returned to Jerusalem to preach Christ there, it is the Hellenists – the Greek-speaking Jews – who plot to kill him (9:29).

It is appropriate for the Acts scenario of the spread of the gospel that Paul leaves Jerusalem for the thoroughly hellenized city of Caesarea, and from there goes off to Tarsus, a major centre of Stoic learning and a thoroughly hellenized city (9:30). In all three of the Acts' accounts of Paul's conversion, the divine purpose behind this event is said to be the outreach to the Gentiles, although the Jews are to be hearers of the gospel as well. In 9:15, Paul is to carry the Lord's name to "the Gentiles and kings and the sons of Israel." In 22:21, he is told that he will be sent far away to the Gentiles. In Paul's final biographical apologetic before King Agrippa (26:16–18), he was instructed that God would preserve him from plots and attacks by Jews and Gentiles in order that they might see the truth, turning from darkness to light and "from the power of Satan", receiving forgiveness, and finding their place among the people of God. Meanwhile, however, the Acts account concentrates on the situation in Palestine, which includes Judaea, Galilee and Samaria, where the church is built up in peace, enjoys the encouragement of the Holy Spirit, and grows in numbers (9:31). The guidelines and the personnel have now been indicated in the Acts narrative whereby the gospel will move out of this initial arena of its impact into the wider world. But up to this point in the Acts account the activity of the apostles and – through them – of the Spirit, is primarily in Jerusalem and the adjacent territory of Judaea. The crucial figure through whom the transition to the wider world will occur is Peter.

2. The Transition Begins through Peter

The Acts narrative describes Peter's visit to the cities of the coastal plain, where miracles performed by him furnish divine approval of this new sphere of activity, attract wide public attention and bring many into the fellowship of the new community: the paralytic in Lydda (8:32–35) and the raising of Dorcas from the dead (8:36–43). This coastal area was strongly influenced by Graeco-Roman culture, but the set piece of Romanization in Palestine was Peter's next destination: Caesarea. With the combined aims of gaining favor with the Roman emperor and imposing Roman culture on the territory he ruled, Herod the Great rebuilt ancient Samaria into a model Graeco-Roman city and renamed it Sebaste (in honor of Augustus). And on the Mediterranean coast adjacent to the region of Samaria he rebuilt Strato's Tower, giving it the name of

Caesarea Maritima. He enlarged the port to facilitate commerce, built an aqueduct to provide the city with an abundance of water and a sewer system. Buildings and streets were laid out symmetrically, with temple, theater, amphitheater, hippodrome and elaborate marketplace – facilities which served for public assembly and entertainment in the Roman fashion. The city was the capital of Roman Palestine for more than six centuries, and became the first target of attack by the Jewish nationalists in the first revolt against Rome in 66 CE. It was there that the Roman military forces were based and administered, so that the name, the culture, the power base in Caesarea symbolized and embodied for Jews in Palestine the cultural, economic and political dominance by a pagan power of the land that they considered to be theirs. It was most fittingly in Caesarea, therefore, that a major shift occurs in the strategy of the apostles to fulfil their commission by the risen Jesus. The Acts account shows how difficult it was for Peter to get the message as to how he was to approach a Roman military officer in the name of Christ.

Cornelius' credentials as an agent of Roman power and presence are impeccable: he is the centurion of the Italian Cohort.[7] In several important ways, Cornelius was prepared for the transitional role that Acts describes him as fulfilling. Although we are not told specifically that the focus of his devotion was the God of Israel, that is implied in the terminology used in Acts 10:2: he was devout (*eusebes*) and feared God, gave alms to the people generously and prayed constantly to God (8:2). He probably represents a significantly large group of Gentiles who were drawn to the Jewish understanding of God as one, imageless and morally-demanding, but who did not accept circumcision and thereby become a proselyte.[8] H.J. Cadbury noted long ago that the terminology in Acts shifts from the more Semitic "God-fearer" to "God-worshipper" when the story shifts its locale from primarily Jewish to primarily Gentile settings.[9] Cornelius carried with him in his religious interests his entire household. This pattern of conversion of households appears elsewhere in Acts as well.

Characteristic of the modes of divine direction and communication in Luke-Acts, an angel tells Cornelius where to find "Simon who is called Peter" in Joppa. Peter, prepared by a vision (as we noted in the previous chapter) is "inwardly perplexed" (10:17), but having had the experience three times

in a row of the celestial bedsheet with assorted birds, reptiles
and animals and the orders to eat, is ready to accept the
invitation to visit Cornelius when the messengers arrive. The
description of Cornelius that his emissaries offer to Peter is
important for the theme under discussion here: Cornelius is
righteous and fears God, and is attested as such "by the whole
nation of the Jews" (10:22). On arrival in Caesarea, Peter is
met by Cornelius, his friends and relatives (10:24). Upon
entering Cornelius' home, Peter is initially embarrassed by his
host's prostrating himself, and then articulates the norm of
Jewish covenantal identity: that it is contrary to established
principle for any Jew to associate with or enter the abode of
someone of another nation. Significantly, the term used here,
athemitos, is not found in connection with the law or the
prophets in the Old Testament or the New Testament, but
occurs in the LXX only in the late writings, II and III Macca-
bees.[10] The only other appearance of the word in the New
Testament (I Peter 4:3) speaks of idolatry and immoral actions
as lawless, without designation of the laws involved. The
allusion in Acts 10:28 to Mosaic law is not ruled out, but the
characteristic term for that law in both the gospels and the
letters of Paul, *nomos*, is supplanted here in Acts by the
much more general hellenistic term, *athemitos*, which means,
"contrary to correct principle". The adjustment even to hellenistic language is accordingly evident.

In Pharisaic understanding of maintenance of purity of
God's people, to enter the house of anyone who did not
observe the ritual requirements, and above all to share a meal
with such a one, was to forfeit one's own purity until proper
atonement and purification were ritually restored. Peter's
conviction overturns these purity principles, however. Further, he attributes this basic shift in point of view to God, who
has told him not to call *anyone* – Jew or Gentile, ritually pure
or not – "profane or unclean" (10:28). What is depicted here is
a radical change in the specification of criteria for participation
in the people of God. Confronted by this challenge to traditional Jewish understanding of purity, Peter found himself
with no counter-argument (10:29).

After hearing from Cornelius how he had been led to ask
Peter to come to his house, Peter addresses those gathered.
His opening statement is a declaration of God's concern for
and openness to people from any nation who are willing to hear

and obey his word. Putting the issue succinctly concerning the relationship of Israel to the new community he speaks of the word which God "sent to Israel, preaching good news of peace by Jesus Christ" (10:36). Once more, the primary attention is on what Jesus did "both in the country of the Jews and in Jerusalem" (10:39). The summary of the sermon concludes with the declaration that the exalted Jesus is "ordained by God to be the judge of the living and the dead" (10:43). That this is not limited to Israel becomes explicit in the final declaration that forgiveness of sins through his name is available to "every one who believes in his name" (10:43). As we noted earlier, confirmation of this open invitation is provided by God through the outpouring of the Spirit "on *all* who heard the word" (10:44).

As though this dramatic scene were not sufficiently potent to convey the message of the open invitation across ethnic and ritual boundaries, the theme is articulated in 11:1, where the apostles and Jerusalem-based Christians hear about the Gentiles having accepted "the word of God". Then the story is told by Peter in Jerusalem, under direct challenge from those who want to insist on circumcision as a prerequisite for covenantal participation (11:2–3). It is not Peter but God who lays down the basic principle about separating humanity into groups on the basis of ritual or dietary regulations: "What God has cleansed you must not call profane" (11:9). This was confirmed by the Spirit, who told Peter to go to the house of Cornelius, "making no distinction" on ethnic or purity grounds (11:12). With the Spirit poured out on these non-law-observant Gentiles, Peter asks, "Who was I that I could withstand God?" (11:17) . The apostles agree with Peter's estimate of what has happened: God has granted repentance and new life to the Gentiles (11:18). The basis is now established for further outreach across the traditional boundaries that marked off the covenant people of Israel.

3. Wider Outreach: Geographically, Ethnically and Culturally

As a consequence of the persecution of Christians in Jerusalem in connection with the martyrdom of Stephen, fugitives from Jerusalem went as far as Phoenicia, Cyprus and Antioch. Initially they confined their witness concerning Jesus to Jewish hearers, but some from Cyprus and the coast of north Africa (Cyrene) began preaching about Jesus to Greeks (11:19–20). The results were remarkable in that "a great number" joined the new fellowship. Barnabas, sent by the Jerusalem apostles to investigate and evaluate what was reported to have occurred not only approves this outreach but furthers it by his own effective preaching to Gentiles, with the result that "a large company was added to the Lord" (11:24). With the help of Paul, who was brought from Tarsus for this purpose, the large membership of the community in Antioch receives instruction for an entire year (11:25–26). Evangelism of Gentiles is now supplemented and built up through the teaching activity of Paul and Barnabas.

Tangible evidence of the mutual concern between the pioneer community in the center of Judaism, Jerusalem, and this mix of Jews and Gentiles in a major Graeco-Roman center, Antioch, is provided through the contribution sent to the faithful who lived in Judaea (11:27–30).[11] Mention of the link with Jerusalem provides the occasion for the author of Acts to describe what is happening to the community there while the gospel is starting its path across the Roman world. Herod Agrippa attacks the church there, executing its leader, James the son of Zebedee (12:1–2), and imprisoning Peter. Peter is freed from prison by an angel of the Lord, to the astonishment of the Christians gathered there for prayer (12:2–17). God punishes Herod for his blasphemous self-esteem, as we have noted. Continuity between the Jerusalem community and the mission about to be launched from Antioch is embodied by John Mark,[12] whose mother had hosted the gathering at which the divinely liberated Peter miraculously arrived (12:12). The simultaneous extension and transformation of what began in Jerusalem continue to be the central themes of Acts.

The mixed membership of the leadership circle of the church in Antioch is made explicit in Acts 13:1. Included are Barnabas (a Jew from Jerusalem, assigned to Antioch by the apostles), Symeon, called "Black" (semitic in name, but perhaps ethnically of black origin), Lucius of Cyrenaica (a Roman name, from north Africa, where there was a large Jewish population), Manaen (a transliteration of the semitic, Menachem; *syntrophos* suggests an intimate friend from childhood of Herod Antipas). All are characterized as "prophets and teachers" – across regional, ethnic, political, and ritual boundaries. They are instructed by God through the Spirit to designate Barnabas and (the late-comer) Paul for the next phase of the outreach of the good news to the ends of the earth (13:1-3).

The strategy of Paul and Barnabas on their wider mission continues to be to go first to the gatherings of Diaspora Jews in the various cities of the empire, beginning at Salamis on Cyprus and then across the island (13:5-6).The Roman consul resident in Paphos summoned the itinerant messengers of the gospel to come to him because "he was seeking to hear the word of God" (13:8). In passing, the author of Acts characterizes him as "a man of understanding". His perception is demonstrated when a Jewish false prophet (Bar Jesus, also known as Elymas) is unsuccessful in diverting the consul from the faith (13:8). His conviction of the truth of the apostles' message is confirmed when he witnesses the punitive miracle performed by Saul in blinding the magician. Acts reports that he "was astonished at the teaching of the Lord", although it is no indication as to the content of what he was taught. The main point is that through such a miracle God provides confirmation for the truth of the message and for the strategy which it declares it to one who earlier would have seemed a totally unlikely and wholly inappropriate prospect: an official of the Roman government.

The same strategy for proclamation of the gospel is evident when the apostles reach Antioch-in-Pisidia (13:13-41). Paul's[13] sermon in the synagogue there focusses on the history of Israel, but it emphasizes that its origins were outside the land of Canaan, which was not Israel's ancestral land but was given to the nation by God for a period of time prior to the establishment of the monarchy under Saul. Israel's savior has now come – Jesus – and is a descendant of David. As we noted in Chapter 2, the promises made to David of a unique son, of one who would triumph over death, were not fulfilled in the person of David or in his era. Rather, they are now being fulfilled through Jesus of Nazareth. Through him forgiveness of sins is proclaimed and everyone who trusts in him, whether Jew or Gentile, is freed from the law of Moses. Those who scorn this message are depicted by Paul as fulfilling the prophetic warning of Habbakuk about the disbelief that will greet the great work that God will one day do in their midst (13:41 = Hab. 1:5). The people as a whole are eager to hear more of the message, and already many Jews and pious proselytes become followers of Paul and hence of the new community where they can "continue in the grace of God" (13:43).

The success of the proclamation of the gospel is so great that two kinds of reaction take place. "Almost the whole city" – which would be predominantly Gentile hearers – came together on the following sabbath to hear the word of God. It is noteworthy, however, that it was on the Jewish holy day that this great congregation occurred. The Jewish leaders were aware of the implications of this reaction to the revised version of God's word to his covenant people, and were understandably troubled by this phenomenal response among Jews and Gentiles to the new message. Hence they sought to discredit both Paul and what he had to say as a message from God (13:44–45). Once more, their adverse attitude is seen by Paul and Barnabas to be in fulfilment of scripture, and they quote Isa. 49:6 (= Acts 13:47). The bringing of light to the Gentiles is declared to be in fulfilment of God's purpose in the world, not contrary to it as the Jewish opponents of the gospel represent. The Jews are to have the priority in hearing the message, but since their leaders reject it and judge themselves "unworthy of eternal life", the apostles now turn to the Gentiles. Salvation will now go out "to the uttermost parts of the earth". The Gentiles, on hearing this prognosis, rejoice and glorify the word of the Lord. Not all who hear the word believe, however: faith is limited to those who are "ordained to eternal life". At the same time, the Jewish leaders arouse the local Gentile city officials to the point that a persecution is instigated against Paul and Barnabas – a clear portent of the opposition that Paul will confront on his return to Jerusalem for the last time and the martyrdom that awaits him in Rome (Acts 21–28). Those who have joined the new community and are left behind when the apostles flee are filled with joy and the Holy Spirit, not because the apostles left but because they have gained a new sense of identity and relationship with God (13:51). Thus the confirming and sustaining power of God through the Spirit marks each stage in the spread of the gospel and the new people of God.

At Iconium there are results similar to those in Pisidian Antioch: Some Jews and Gentiles are converted, while others mount opposition and drive them from the area (14:1–7). At Lystra, however, a new kind of response and a new difficulty emerge when Paul preaches and heals there: Barnabas and Paul are acclaimed as the Greek gods in human form, Zeus and Hermes (14:8–18). The priest of Zeus is ready to offer sacrifice to them as the gods in their midst. The conviction among the Greeks that the gods did come into the human situation and confer benefits, such as healing, was widespread, and these two wonder-workers were likely candidates for those roles. What is implicit here is one of the difficulties that the messengers of the gospel encountered in preaching about Jesus in a Greek culture. The wide popular acclaim of the apostles on what they regard as wholly inappropriate grounds is further complicated when Paul begins to describe the divine ordering of the universe and the providential provision for the sustaining of human life (14:15–17). Paul's use of the concepts of natural law as maintaining the natural and social systems of the world are wholly compatible with Stoic philosophy and serve to enhance the esteem with which these two messengers of Christ are greeted in a sophisticated hellenistic urban setting. Their message, or more accurately, the rhetorical introduction to their message, only increases the popular opinion that these two strangers among them are gods in disguise. In these details of his narrative the author of Acts shows that he perceives certain basic elements which are shared by the view of God and the world proclaimed by Paul and his associates with the cosmic concepts expressed in such a hellenistic philosophy as that of the Stoics. A similar experience will soon be described by him in his story of Paul in Athens (Acts 17). The Jewish opponents foment broad popular opposition to Paul, who is attacked by a mob and left for dead outside the city. He recovers, however, and with Barnabas retraces his route through the cities of southern Asia Minor. At Derbe, the preaching of the gospel results in the conversion of many to discipleship (14:21). The members of the community in each place that they re-visit are given encouragement, instruction, but also warning about the difficulties they face because of their commitment to Christ (14:21–22). A new feature (to be discussed in Chapter 7) is the appointment of elders in each church, and the ceremony of prayer and fasting which accompanied their assignment to this role.

Acts 15 is literarily, conceptually, and theologically the midpoint of the book. The progress of the gospel to the ends of the earth is recessed temporarily so that the issues involved can be made explicit, debated and a defensible conclusion reached. It is wholly in keeping with the strategy of Acts that the discussion of the issue and the official resolution take place in Jerusalem. The issue was raised in Antioch by some Christians from Judaea, who asserted that all males must be circumcized if they are to be saved (15:1). Paul and Barnabas set out for Jerusalem, where the issue is to be raised and a common decision reached by the "apostles and elders" there (15:2). Significantly, they hear reports in Phoenicia and Samaria that Gentiles are being converted and they observe the joy of the community that this inclusive growth of the church is taking place (15:3).

On their arrival in Jerusalem, the cordiality of the welcome is offset by the intransigent position adopted by members of the community there who have brought over their Pharisaic convictions into their new covenantal association in the church. They insist on circumcision for all male Christians (15:4–5). Peter articulates what becomes the official apostolic policy. It was through him that Gentiles had heard the word, and God gave them the Spirit and cleansed their hearts without reference to their conformity to the Mosaic law. To insist on conformity to this basic legal requirement of circumcision puts God to the test, since he welcomed the Gentiles without reference to legal demands, and it ignores the fact that Jews have historically not been able to bear the weight of them either (15:10). All humanity is the potential beneficiary of the unmerited blessing of God through the Lord Jesus (15:11). The validity of this point of view is reinforced when Barnabas and Paul report the signs and wonders which "God had done through them among the Gentiles" (15:12).

James formulates his position on the issue of the grounds of Gentile inclusion in the covenant people. In a mosaic of quotations from the prophets,[14] which we noted briefly in Chapter 3, James sets in a cosmic theological-historical context the development of the inclusion of Gentiles which Peter reported and which is now taking place in the areas visited by Barnabas and Saul. There is an eschatological dimension to what is taking place: it is at some time later than that of the prophet – "after these things" – that God will resume his action in the world. The aim of this divine activity is the rebuilding of the structure through which God's chosen agent exercises rule in God's behalf. The Davidic monarchy has long ago disappeared; the new rule of God is about to be established. Omitted by the author of Acts from his quotation of Amos' prophecy is the phrase found in both the Hebrew text and in the LXX which declares that the kingdom will be restored "just like the days of old" (Amos 9:11). What is happening is seen as transformation rather than merely restoration of the Israelite monarchy. Further, the Hebrew text promises that the Davidic heir will *possess* "what is left of Edom and of all the nations who were once named as mine".[15] Other modifications in the LXX text increase the appropriateness of the quotation for the purpose it serves in Acts. The LXX of Amos 9:12 may be rendered literally, "So that the rest of humanity and all the nations upon whom my name is called upon them may seek" [no object expressed]. The point is that the nations which belong to God will begin to inquire about him. The version given in Acts 15:17 reads instead, "so that the rest of humanity *shall seek the Lord*". The rest of the quotation follows the LXX, including the underscoring of the assertion that it is the Lord who is doing these things. The added phrase from Second Isaiah, however, makes the point that what is happening in the extending of an invitation to the Gentiles to share in the new structure that God is building is no innovation, but has been "made known by God since long ago" (15:18). That factor is underscored in 15:21, where James declares that the Gentiles should have known the basic requirements which he is now making of them, because "from early generations Moses has had in every city those who preach him".

The requirements laid down by James for Gentile Christians have been variously understood by modern interpreters. If we follow that tradition of the Greek New Testament text which omits the phrase "and from what is strangled", the remaining three obligations do not involve the mosaic law specifically: abstinence from idolatry, from sexual impropriety, and from murder (= shedding of blood). If "from what is strangled" is taken as part of the original text, however, then it links naturally with the final phrase "and from blood" to constitute a pair of minimal ritual requirements: Gentile Christians should avoid eating meat when the animal was put to death by strangling[16] or if all the blood was not first removed (Gen. 9:4; Lev. 17:10–16). If these two stipulations were part of the original text of Acts, then the author viewed the Jerusalem council's guidelines as a kind of minimal compromise, according to which certain dietary features were to be observed by Gentile Christians to avoid offending Jewish Christians, or causing any of the latter to refuse to share meals with their Gentile Christian sisters and brothers. As we have noted, Paul acknowledges no such compromise with Jewish legal requirements in his report of the conversation in Galatians 2:1–10 with the apostles in Jerusalem. In any case, the circumcision requirement – which was the occasion for the issue having been raised in Jerusalem – was not imposed on Gentile believers, nor were other ritual or dietary obligations as required by the law of Moses. The importance of this group decision for the author of Acts is underscored in Acts by his further report of the corporate apostolic judgment being put in written form. Addressed to the members "who are of the Gentiles in Antioch and Syria and Cilicia", it includes a summary of the conclusions, commends Paul and Barnabas, and is despatched along with official representatives of the Jerusalem leadership group (15:22). The delegates from Jerusalem demonstrate concretely their approval of the mixed congregation in Antioch in that they themselves take part in the edification and instruction of the Gentile Christians there (15:32).

4. Christian Encounter with Graeco-Roman Religion, Philosophy and Political Order

Chapter 16 of Acts marks a major transition in the progress of the gospel, and does so in at least two dimensions. The scene shifts from the eastern Mediterranean world and predominantly Jewish audiences for Paul and his associates to the mainland of Europe and various forms of engagement with Roman culture. The brief narrative about Paul's choice of Timothy as a co-worker offers symbolism of both continuity and change. With a Jewish mother (now a Christian) and a Gentile father, Timothy is circumcised on Paul's initiative in order to minimize offending potential Jewish hearers (16:1–3). Yet as the party revisits the cities where communities had been founded earlier by Paul and his associates, reports are made in each place of the decisions reached by the apostolic leaders in Jerusalem about the obligations of Gentile believers. The membership of the communities is said to increase daily (16:4–5).

Prevented by the Spirit from visiting the north eastern provinces of Asia Minor, and inspired by a vision, Paul decides that God is calling him to preach the good news in Macedonia. The symbolism involved here is powerful. Paul's point of departure is Troas, or Troy, which was the place of origin of the founders of Rome according to ancient tradition, as celebrated in the *Aeneid* of Virgil. Macedonia was the power base for the takeover of the Greek world by Philip, whose son, Alexander the Great launched a world empire from there. Paul's primary destination is the Roman provincial capital, Philippi, named for the founder of the mixed military and cultural thrust known as hellenization. The first persons indicated as having been contacted by Paul is a group of Jewish women gathered at a meeting place, *proseuche*,[17] on a riverbank outside the city (16:11–13). The most interested listener was a businesswoman, Lydia, whose occupation was selling purple goods, which were colored with an expensive dye made from a type of shellfish. She was a worshipper of the God of Israel, though not a full member of the covenant people (16:14). When she was moved by the Lord to believe what Paul declared, both she and her household were baptized. Group commitments rather than individual decisions were standard in the growth of the church as Acts describes it. A pattern is now set for proclaiming the gospel across geographical, cultural, ethnic, social, economic and sexual boundaries. The implications of this broad propagation of the movement are faced by Paul and his associates as they move from city to city in Macedonia and other districts of Greece.

The unwanted public acclaim of Paul and his co-workers by the young woman with the oracular power leads him to exorcise the spirit from her. She had been daily identifying them as "servants of the Most High God" (16:17). The term, *hypsistos*, appears in both pagan hellenistic inscriptions and literature with reference to Zeus or other pagan deities, as well as in the LXX. It is the regular translation into Greek for the Semitic term for God *elyon*. In Sirach, for which there is no ancient complete Hebrew copy, *hypsistos* occurs 44 times, always with reference to the God of Israel.[18] It was also used by Jews or Christians in speaking of Most High God to serve an apologetic end: the deity whom pagans designated by this superlative epithet is the God of Israel and the God of Jesus Christ. At the same time, the demons are reported in the synoptic tradition to have called Jesus "son of the Most High God" (Mark 5:7; Luke 8:28), just as here the soothsaying woman calls the apostles "servants of the Most High God". In his gospel, Luke has used this term with reference to the God of Israel in the infancy stories (1:32, 76) and in his version of the reward for loving one's enemies: "You will be children of the Most High" (Luke 6:35). The ambivalence of the term provides the occasion for Paul to expel the demon that enables the woman to utter her oracles: "in the name of Jesus Christ" (Acts 16:18).

The response of the owners is to try to punish the apostles for having deprived them of this important source of revenue. But their charge before the civil authorities goes beyond this issue: the accusation is that Paul and his associates are disturbing the city and advocating customs which it is unlawful for Romans to accept or practice (16:20–21). The threat which the Christian movement was perceived as constituting in the second century CE is already articulated here. Accordingly, they are turned over to the mob for corporal punishment, and then placed in prison (16:22–23). When an earthquake shakes the foundations of the prison, opening all the doors and unfastening all the fetters, the jailer is about to commit suicide, on the assumption that all the prisoners in his charge have fled (16:25–27). Capitalizing on the multiple meaning of the jailer's question as to how he might be delivered from the professional crisis in which he has been placed ("What must I do to be saved?"), Paul informs him that trust in the Lord Jesus will save him and his entire household (16:30–31). The jailer gives public testimony to his conversion by accepting baptism at the hands of the apostles, and they show their acceptance of him by sharing a meal. The household rejoices over his faith in God (16:32–34). Yet one more step is depicted in the penetration of the Roman people and their power structure by the good news of Jesus Christ.

Acts does not rest content to report the deliverance of Paul from the political authorities, however. The local authorities had beaten Paul and Silas without a proper trial and in spite of the fact that both of them were Roman citizens. The incident is so severe a violation of both the privileges of Roman citizenship and of due judicial process that Paul refuses to leave the prison quietly and without public attention. The police officials apologize and ask them to leave the prison and the city – which they do (16:35–40). The point is made in Acts thereby that there is no basic conflict between the Roman system – both its citizenship structure and its legal processes – and the faith of the new community. Stated negatively, Christians are not political subversives but deserve the protection of Roman civil law.

A similar crisis over the same basic issue is described as occurring in Thessalonica as well (17:1–9). As usual, Paul is seen here as going first to the Jews in the synagogue, where he seeks to persuade them from the scriptures that Jesus is the Messiah, that he had to suffer and that God has vindicated him by raising him from the dead. Among those persuaded were some Jews, but "a great many of the devout Greeks and not a few of the leading women". The ethnically and socially mixed pattern of participation in the new community is evident once more, and the reaction of some of the Jews is to bring public charges against the apostles for "turning the world upside down", violating Roman law and claiming that there is another king than Caesar: Jesus. The pattern of confrontation between the movement and the political structure of Rome is once more evident, and for the author of Acts will reach its climax in the arrest and extradition to Rome of Paul. It is only when Jason – host to Paul and Silas and apparently to the synagogue which met in his house – pays the local officials the appropriate security fee that the apostles are freed. Moving on to Beroea, the apostles find a more eager audience in the synagogue, where many are converted, including more wealthy women (17:10–15). The distinctive role of women in the Jesus movement and in the spread of Christianity throughout the empire is a consistent theme in both Luke and Acts. With mounting Jewish opposition, Paul moves on to Athens, leaving behind in Thessalonica Silas and Timothy.

It is in Athens that the author of Acts gives the most extensive account of the encounter between the message of Christ and the wisdom of the Greeks. Offended by the multitude of idols he saw in the city, Paul divides his time between debates in the synagogue with Jews and devout Gentiles and public declamation of the gospel in that great center of commerce and common life, the Agora. His message was greeted by local Stoic and Epicurean philosophers as though he were rummaging through trash. Others, misunderstanding his claims about the risen Christ, thought he was promulgating a religion with a

new male/female pair of divinities like Adonis and Venus or
Osiris and Isis: Jesus and Anastasia (= resurrection). Taken to
the Areopagus, where the civic council on intellectual matters
convened regularly, Paul is invited to explain what this new
teaching of his is.

His address begins with highest praise for the Athenians:
by every criterion they are very religious people (17:22). As he
was passing through the city, observing their sacred places
and objects, he saw an altar with an inscription, "To an
unknown god".[19] Making a kind of pun on the Greek word
agnostos, he says that they are actually honoring the unknown
god, since they are worshipping him without knowing who
he is. The critique of locating deity in idols or shrines was
wholly compatible with Stoic teaching, although it would have
raised major difficulties for Jews who thought God dwelt in
the temple in Jerusalem (17:24). God does not need human
offerings, but provides life and breath, habitation, time frame
for the whole human race, which is seen as basically one
(17:25–26). The appropriate human response to this ordered
and ordering deity is to seek to know him, while recognizing
that God is the one in whom all human beings exist (17:27–28).
This insight is confirmed by quotations, not from the Jewish
scriptures but from pagan poets who affirm that god is the
locus and origin of all human life (17:28). In the true religion
there is no place for idolatry or for identifying deity with any
tangible thing. Rather, the religious obligation of men and
women is to look to the standards of their mode of life,
conscious that God will call them to account (17:29–30). Up to
this point, what Paul is reported as saying has its counterpart in
the writings of the middle and later Stoics, such as Posidonius
(135–50 BCE) and Seneca (4 BCE–65 CE),[20] with the emphasis on
the divine penetration and ordering of the creation, and the
ultimate divine judgment of humanity. Furthermore, the basic
pattern of creation, preservation and redemption set out in the
Areopagus address is to be found in Jewish and early Christian
writings as well.[21] These include The Sibylline Oracles, I
Clement, Apostolic Constitutions, Prayer of Manasseh. Paul
is pictured here as establishing as broad a common ground
as possible with his hearers, regardless of their religious
background. The crucial shift in Paul's argument comes at
verse 31, where the criterion for human accountability is not
law – either Stoic natural law or Jewish revealed law – but

a human being marked out by God, the unnamed Jesus. Confidence in this claim has been divinely provided, in that God has raised him from the dead.

The strategy of this address is remarkable. The choice of Stoic principles as a point of entry and the quotation of familiar Greek writers virtually guarantees attention and a sympathetic hearing – at least initially. The degree of overlap between the concepts in this popular philosophy and what the author regards as the basic Christian worldview is striking, and serves the reader as a demonstration of what can be done in approaching with the gospel those who have no familiarity with the teachings of the Jewish scriptures. The results are reportedly mixed, ranging from intellectual scorn, through expressions of interest in further information, to faith on the part of a group of unspecified size, only two of whom are named. That one of the latter is a woman – apparently pagan and willing to appear in public at such a gathering – and that the other, Dionysus, was a member of this august intellectual body is in itself significant. The names indicate how the gospel was able to penetrate an alien culture and evoke a response of faith when a suitable method of approach was employed.

5. Mounting Tensions with Civil Authorities and Established Cultural Institutions

On arrival in Corinth, Paul's initial tactics resemble those he exercised in other cities of the eastern Mediterranean: seek to persuade Jews gathered in their synagogues. His aides there are a Jewish couple, Aquila and Priscilla; from Pontus in eastern Asia Minor, they had been living in Rome. It was there, presumably, that they had been converted to faith in Jesus as the Christ. Their expulsion from Rome under the emperor Claudius along with the Jewish community there was almost certainly the result of the penetration of the gospel among the Jews in the capital city.[22] Paul's audience in the synagogue presumably includes both Jews and seeking Gentiles as did Aquila's hearers there (18:1–4). But it is to the Jews who turn against him so vehemently that he announces a shift from Jews to Gentiles as the primary focus of his mission (18:6). That takes place literally when he moves to the house of Titius Justus, which is next to the place where the synagogue met. Ironically, after the shift of location, Crispus, the head of the synagogue, is converted with his household and join the Christian community in Corinth (18:7–8). In Ephesus he is twice reported as preaching in the synagogue (18:19; 19:8), so that he is not seen as having abandoned the Jews as potential members of the new community. Other evidence of the cultural transition that the movement is undergoing is to be seen in the instruction that must be given to a native Alexandrian who had been "instructed in the way of the Lord", who practiced the baptism of John and knew the scriptures well, but did not know anything about the baptism of the Spirit. This Jewish native of that strongly hellenized city bore the name of a Greek deity, Apollo. Instructed by Priscilla and Aquila, he is able to argue effectively with Jewish antagonists that Jesus is the Messiah (18:24–28). Similarly in Ephesus Paul must enable the believers to move beyond the baptism of John to baptism in the name of Jesus, with the accompanying outpouring of the Spirit and the charismatic manifestation in tongues and prophecy (19:1–6). As in Corinth, the first arena for procla-mation of the gospel in Ephesus is the synagogue, but follow-ing mounting Jewish opposition there, a public hall is hired, in much the same way that philosophical instruction of Stoic or Epicurean variety in the Graeco-Roman world would be propagated in publicly available lecture halls (19:8–10).

An important precedent is set at this point in terms of the developing Acts narrative: what is at issue between Paul and his Jewish detractors is a matter of their laws, not violations of Roman laws or religious customs. Gallio refuses to take action against the movement – which is a significant pattern to refer to when, in the early second century, Christians do come under imperial scrutiny as a potentially subversive movement (18:12–17). Acts complicates the picture of the relationship of the Christian movement to Jewish norms for covenantal identity, however, when it twice depicts Paul as cutting his hair in fulfilment of a Jewish ascetic vow first in Corinth (18:18) and then in Jerusalem (20:20–26). His fidelity to Jewish law and tradition is an essential and recurrent feature of the series of apologies Acts reports him as offering at the hearings before the civil and religious authorities in Jerusalem and Caesarea (Acts 21–25).

Another type of cultural adjustment is described as occurring in Ephesus, when crowds are attracted by the healings and exorcisms performed through Paul (19:11–20). Jewish exorcists are punished for exploiting the name of Jesus to expel evil spirits, and many magicians are converted, praising the name of Jesus and destroying their books of magical formulae. The attention this attracted publicizes further the name of Jesus and the word of the Lord. The negative response to the power of the gospel in attracting throngs of followers is apparent when a campaign to discredit Paul before the civil authorities is mounted by the silversmiths of Ephesus who manufacture images of Artemis, the goddess honored in the world-renowned temple there. It is significant that among those seeking to protect Paul from the attack of the hostile mob are some Asiarchs (19:31). These were men of wealth and power chosen by cities across Asia Minor to represent them on the council of the province[23] – astonishing persons to serve as supporters of Paul and the gospel. The town clerk comes to their defense, pointing out that the charges against Paul and his followers are unsupported and that there is an established legal process if they have instigated civil disobedience or violated the laws of the state. It is his opinion, however, that the accused "are neither sacrilegious nor blasphemers" of Artemis. The town assembly, not an impromptu mob scene, is the place to air such complaints. It is the accusers, not the accused, who are violating the public peace. The author of Acts is obviously making a case for due process to be observed when charges are made against the Christians.

Similar unfounded charges are brought against Paul in the Jerusalem temple by Jews from Asia (21:27): that he has violated the sanctity of the temple by bringing an unclean Gentile into its courts (21:28). Protected by the Roman soldiers from the violence of the Jewish crowd, Paul is taken into custody (21:35). The Roman tribune mistakenly links Paul with a revolt organized by an Egyptian (21:38). The charge provides Paul an opportunity to offer a public defense in which he affirms that his Jewish credentials are impeccable (22:1–5). In the process he affirms that he is also a Roman citizen and therefore protected by due legal process (21:39; 22:25–29). The tribune seeks to discover the real reason for Jewish hostility toward Paul (22:30), which provides another occasion for a Pauline apology in which it is shown that the real violator of Jewish law is the high priest (23:3) and that his own views are firmly within the Pharisaic tradition, especially as concerns belief in the resurrection – a statement which elicits support for him from the Pharisees (23:6–9). In the series of apologies which occupy the next three chapters of Acts, the basic themes recur: (1) the charges against Paul are brought by Jewish opponents, and are based on their interpretation of the Jewish scriptures; (2) the Romans at every time in the past have protected Paul, recognizing that he has not violated Roman civil law; (3) Paul has been faithful to the Jewish law and has performed properly in the temple, although he is persuaded that the Jewish scriptures point to Christ. Repeatedly, the corporate judgments of the Roman officials are said to be that by the standards of Roman law, Paul is innocent (25:13–22; 26:31). Significantly, Paul's private defense before Felix and Drusilla is based on Stoic principles of justice, self-control and future judgment (24:25), and was so persuasive that Felix is alarmed that he might be convinced of its truth! There is a subtle but powerful apologetic factor implied in the point that a leader of the young Christian movement will appeal for justice to the head of the pagan state, Caesar (25:8–12). The importance of this feature, with its clear implication for early second-century Christians and non-Christians that Christianity is not politically subversive, is underscored by the repetition of this appeal: 25:21; 26:32; 28:19. The divine sanction for this appeal is given in the description of the angelic vision that came to Paul in the midst of the protracted storm at sea: "Do not be afraid, Paul: you must stand before Caesar" (27:24).

The vivid narratives and eloquent discourses which bring the book to a close make the point that the mission of the gospel to the Gentiles is fully in accord with the Jewish scriptures (26:19–23). The Roman authorities must intervene once more in order to save Paul from the attack of his Jewish opponents (27:43). God's support for Paul and protection of him are evident in the story of the viper's bite, which proves to be harmless (28:1–6). In Rome the authorities permit Paul to dwell in private quarters, with a military guard – presumably more for protection from his enemies than to keep him under arrest (28:16). There is said to be no ground for either Jewish religious or Roman civil charges that have been made against Paul. Even the disbelief of the Jews is in fulfilment of their scriptures (28:23–28). Meanwhile, at the political and symbolic centre of the pagan world there dwells Paul, the pre-eminent messenger of the gospel to the Gentiles. He lives there with the permission and protection of Roman authority to which he had appealed in order to achieve justice in the face of accusations brought against him (28:19–20). And he works there among Gentiles who are receptive to his message about Jesus as Lord and Christ (28:28): "Let it be known to you that this salvation of God has been sent to the Gentiles: they will listen."

5

Structure and Strategy in the New Community

1. The Leadership Structure

1.1 *The Apostles*

Although the traditional title for this New Testament book, The Acts of the Apostles, does not convey the range of interests and themes presented in it, it is not an inappropriate name for the work. The launching and supervision of the community reaching out into the wider Roman world is the work of the apostles, although they recede in importance as the story progresses.

Since the English word, apostle, is no more than a transliteration of the Greek original, *apostolos*, it conveys nothing of the significance of the term. What is essential is to see the connotations of the cognate verb, *apostello*, as it appears in Acts. What is evident is that this verb is used by the author to describe God's guidance of the history of his people and especially of those who are chosen and empowered by God to carry out his purpose in the world. This understanding is vividly set forth in Peter's address to the crowd in Solomon's Portico of the temple (Acts 3). Here both the initial coming of the "child" Jesus and his eschatological appearance at the end of the age are described as God's *sending* of Jesus (3:20–26). And that sending is aimed initially at those who are the children of the prophets *and of the covenant*, which is ultimately to include as beneficiaries of the divine blessing promised to Abraham "all the families of the earth". It is this divine redemptive purpose which is being achieved by God's sending of Jesus, just as earlier he sent Joseph to Egypt and then sent Moses to lead Israel out of Egypt (7:34–35). Now God's word has been sent to Israel through Jesus (10:36). That work continues through Jesus, who sent Ananias to accost Saul (8:17) in preparation for his call to be messenger to the Gentiles (26:17). Similarly, the Spirit tells Peter that he has sent three men from Cornelius to invite Peter to visit this Gentile and thereby to launch the mission of the gospel beyond ethnic Israel. It is a wholly fitting summary with which the author of Acts brings this book to a close: "Let it be known to you that this salvation of God has been *sent* to the Gentiles: they will listen" (28:28).

It is the risen Jesus who chooses the apostles (1:2) and commissions them to carry out their divinely designed role as witnesses to him "to the end of the earth" (1:8). They are given instruction through the Spirit and soon to be empowered through the Spirit to carry out their task. The primary prerequisite for this role is that they have seen Jesus risen from the dead, and Acts makes the emphatic point that he offered them many proofs that he had been raised from the dead and did so over a period of forty days. In the concluding chapter of his gospel Luke has indicated that the risen Jesus enabled his followers to understand "in all the scriptures the things concerning himself" (Luke 24:27,45) and he became known to them "in the breaking of bread" (24:35). It is the outpouring of the Spirit, however, which is to provide the enabling power by which their testimony is to be launched on a potentially worldwide scale (Acts 1:8).

The importance of the apostles' having been with Jesus from the day of his baptism until his ascension is repeated when it comes to choosing a successor for Judas (1:22). That the process of choice of Matthias is correct and that it has divine approval is shown in Acts through the references to scripture which are being fulfilled (1:20; Ps. 69:25; 109:8) but especially through the confirmation by the sacred lot. Equally significant is that the number twelve is preserved for the apostolic circle, since in Luke 22:29–30 the symbolic link between the role of the apostles and the destiny of the historic covenant people is made specific: "You shall sit on thrones judging the twelve tribes of Israel."

Further symbolic significance for the role of the apostles is offered in the opening section of Acts through the Pentecost story. As we have noted, the gift of tongues is not here seen as ecstatic speech but as divine enablement to communicate the gospel across linguistic, geographic and cultural boundaries. The rhetorical question of the puzzled onlookers assembled in Jerusalem from around the world is of profound importance for the viewpoint of Acts: "How is it we hear, each in his own native language?" (2:8). Thus the apostles are not only called to a world mission, but enabled by God to fulfil it. Their primary role is to communicate God's word concerning Jesus across these barriers which divide humanity.

The role of the apostles in relation to the new community is conveniently summarized at the end of the Pentecost story (2:42), where we read that the three thousand who responded in faith to the apostles' message "devoted themselves to the apostles' teaching and fellowship, to the breaking of bread and the prayers." The primary tasks of the apostles are seen to be instruction, fostering community, celebrating the eucharist, and leading in prayers. The combination of teaching and preaching is mentioned again in 4:2 in connection with the mounting opposition to the apostles from a coalition of Jewish opponents. The basis of the apostles' instruction and proclamation is said to be "what we have seen and heard" (4:20). Even their detractors, while noting the apostles' lack of education or sophistication, note that "they had been with Jesus" (4:13). Indeed, it is the name of Jesus which they regard as the source of their power (4:10–12). And it is through the name of Jesus that God continues to perform signs and wonders among them "through the name of [God's] holy servant Jesus" (4:29). Because of these modes of confirmation from God, they are bold to continue to speak God's word (4:31).

Throughout Acts, the proclamation of the word is a central concern and the major factor in the spread of the new community. It is in response to the word heard and believed that the group continues to grow by the thousands in Jerusalem (4:4). When the division of labor between the apostles and others in the community occurs in Acts 6 (discussed below), the apostles express the conviction that their primary role is the preaching of the word (6:2). They are to devote themselves to prayer and the ministry of the word (6:4). When the word of God increases, the number of followers multiplies proportionately (6:7). Although the hellenists were assigned initially to "serve tables" (6:2–3), when they fled from Jerusalem, they went about preaching the word (8:4). Their activity and its results were reported to the apostles (8:14) and confirmed by Peter and John, the apostolic investigators (8:14, 25). The word which God initially sent to Israel, "preaching good news of peace by Jesus Christ" (10:36) has now reached out to the non-Jewish world. That God is behind this is confirmed by the outpouring of the Spirit on *all* who heard the word (10:44), and is so reported to the apostles in Jerusalem (11:1). Those driven out of Palestine as a result of the conflict and persecution that arose in connection with Stephen initially preached the word in Antioch only to Jews (11:19). But proclamation to Gentiles was followed by instruction through Paul and Barnabas (11:25–26). In spite of official opposition and intra-Christian disagreement over the inclusion of Gentiles in the covenant people, Acts declares that "the word of God grew and multiplied" (12:24). It is the preaching of this word which is central to the work of Paul throughout Acts, to Jewish and Gentile hearers, before the simple and the mighty, from Antioch to Rome. It is instruction in the word which enables Christians in these various settings to be built up and to share in the inheritance of the saints of God (20:32). These are the primary apostolic tasks.

The opposition from the religious officials which the apostles experience in Jerusalem is no deterrent to their carrying forward their work. It was through the coalition of these civil and religious authorities that the Lord's "Anointed" had been put to death (4:25–27), yet ironically what they achieved was the fulfilment of the predestined plan of God for the redemption of God's people (4:28). The apostles pray, not for relief from oppression and opposition, but for the continuing manifestations through signs and wonders of God's support of what is happening through Jesus. In confirmation of their perception and their prayer, the place is shaken and all are filled with the Holy Spirit (4:31). Similarly, the imprisonment of the apostles by the high priest and his Sadducean colleagues provides the occasion for another sign of God's support: the miraculous release of the apostles from prison (5:17–21). When the prohibition to preach the message about Jesus is uttered by the high priest, the apostles declare that their obedience is to God rather than to the sacerdotal authority and its decree (4:27–31). Again there is irony in that it is a teacher of the law, Gamaliel, who

warns about the possibility that these priestly opponents may
be in fact opposing God in their hostility to the Christian
witnesses (5:33–39). In spite of the beating which follows, the
apostles rejoice in their suffering for the name of Jesus, and
continue in the temple and in homes to proclaim the good
news (5:40–42). Opposition and persecution are not perceived
as signs of divine disapproval, but as participation in the
struggle that must precede the achievement of God's purpose
through the crucified and vindicated Jesus.

The apostles are pictured in Acts as not only messengers,
however, but also as agents of supervision, confirmation and
commissioning. The logic of the opening paragraph of Acts 6
is difficult to follow, probably because there are two factors at
work in the narrative at this point. On the one hand, there
is a tension which arises between "the Hebrew" and "the
Hellenists". This seems to refer to the primary language of the
two groups involved: Hebrew (or Aramaic) and Greek. The
ground of the conflict is said to be that the "widows" of the
Hellenists were neglected "in the daily distribution". What is
being distributed or the nature of the organizational arrange-
ment for the distribution are not specified, but since there is
an immediate reference to "serving tables" (6:2), it appears
that the community pools its resources and gives out food
daily to the poor and the deprived among its members. Both
the noun which describes the distribution (*diakonia*) and the
verb used for serving tables (*diakoneo*) are obviously the etymo-
logical base for the term, deacon, which figures elsewhere in
the New Testament. In the deutero-Pauline literature it has
become a technical term for an office in the church.[1] We shall
discuss this role below, but here it is important to see that the
division of labor as depicted in Acts is a matter, not of distinct
roles for deacons over against apostles, but of different arenas
in which the messengers of Christ operate. All those chosen
by the community to "serve tables" have Greek names, and
what they are soon doing is preaching the gospel to non-Jews.[2]
Once more there is irony in that the role the apostles see for
themselves is the ministry (*diakonia*) of the word (6:4).

The persecution of the church in Jerusalem which followed
on Stephen's defence before the high priest and the council
(Acts 7) resulted in the scattering of the church throughout
Judaea and Samaria, but left the apostles in Jerusalem (8:1).
The proclamation of the gospel to the Samaritans by Philip

receives divine confirmation through the exorcisms and the signs of healing which occur there (8:4–7). The response of the apostles establishes a pattern which recurs through Acts 15: evaluation and confirmation of innovations in the proclamation of the gospel are to be made by the apostles as a kind of ecclesiastical board of control resident in Jerusalem, the place where it all began. The sanction for the apostolic decisions is provided by the outpouring of the Spirit. The report of the conversions in Samaria leads the apostles to despatch – the verb is *apostello*! – Peter and John to inspect on the site what is taking place. Not only do these apostolic delegates give tangible evidence of their approval through the laying on of hands – which is followed by the outpouring of the Spirit – but they themselves engage in preaching in "many villages of the Samaritans" on their way back to Jerusalem (8:25). The movement of the gospel from Judaea and Samaria predicted in Acts 1:8 is in process, and has now received apostolic approval. Similarly, the conversion of Paul and his coming to Jerusalem arouse anxieties among the members of the community there until, on the initiative of Barnabas, Paul is brought before the apostles to confirm the authenticity of his conversion (9:26–27).

The next major step in the spread of the gospel is its proclamation to Gentiles through Peter. The report of what had happened in the household of Cornelius the centurion reached the ears of the apostles in Jerusalem. When Peter returned there he was required to give a detailed report of both his preaching to the Gentiles and of the evidence of divine confirmation of what he had done through the coming of the Spirit on these new believers (11:1–16). Peter describes himself as hard to convince of the appropriateness of what he engaged in, but the Spirit's descent on the converts convinced him that he "could not withstand God" (11:17). His critics are silenced and glorify God because repentance has been granted to the Gentiles (11:18).

The most solemn act of confirmation by the apostles is the corporate decision made by them on the question of what aspects of covenantal requirements deriving from the law of Moses are to be binding on Gentiles who enter the new covenant community (Acts 15). The issue was raised in Antioch, where Paul and Barnabas had reported how God "had opened the door of faith to the Gentiles" (14:27). Visiting Judaean Christians had raised the issue of the necessity of circumcision for covenantal participation (15:1). A group of appointed delegates from the Antioch community, including Paul and Barnabas, are sent off to Jerusalem to confer with "the apostles and elders" on the issue (15:2). En route to Jerusalem, the report of the conversion of the Gentiles brings great joy to believers in Phoenicia and Samaria, and is favorably received in Jerusalem as well (15:3–4). At the instigation of Jewish Christians of Pharisaic background the circumcision issue is raised, and the apostles and elders meet to discuss the question (15:5–6). Peter speaks first, and urges that no ritual requirement be imposed on Gentile believers (15:6–11). The authenticity of the conversion of the Gentiles is confirmed by the signs and wonders which accompanied their response in faith to the gospel (15:12). Finally, James as the spokesman for the apostolic circle articulates the official policy, which is declared to be in accord with the scriptures.[3]

The importance of this council in Jerusalem as an instrument of official policy and action is underscored in Acts by the letter which is despatched to the church in Antioch and by the delegation of "leading men among the brethren" who are chosen to carry the message from the apostles to this church where the issue of Gentile participation has arisen (15:22–29). The bracketing together of "the Holy Spirit and [the apostolic] us" (15:28) is highly significant as an indicator of the crucial role of authority performed by the apostles as Acts perceives it. Analogously, the response of the community in Antioch is described as a formal assembling of the members, the delivery of the letter and its public reading, the joyous reaction to its message and the prophetic exhortation from the apostolic delegates (15:30–34). Local confirmation is provided through the effectiveness of the preaching and teaching activity of Paul and Barnabas and others in Antioch before they set out on the next phase of their wider mission to the Roman world (15:35).

The basic role of the apostles has now been fulfilled as the author of Acts sees it by their approval of the terms of admission of Gentiles to the community of faith. They are not mentioned by title again in Acts. When Paul returns to Jerusalem for the last time, he visits James and "all the elders" (21:18). Reference is made yet once more to the letter in which the corporate decision about Gentile admission to the covenant was formulated (21:25), but from this point on in the Acts narrative Paul's activities in Jerusalem and vicinity are with the civil and religious authorities. The apostolic role in approving the mission to the Gentiles was completed midway through the book of Acts. Another curious feature of Acts in relation to the term, *apostolos*, is that in 14:4 and 14 it is used with reference to Paul and Barnabas. It is their roles as emissaries of the gospel which is in view, however, and not the policy formulation, decision-making, and confirmatory function that Acts sees the Jerusalem apostles as fulfilling.

1.2 Deacons

Although *diakonos* is not used in Acts as a title, the cognate verb *diakoneo* and abstract noun, *diakonia*, appear frequently. As we noted in connection with the appointment of the servers-of-tables in Acts 6, what Stephen and the others do involves far more than that domestic duty. Stephen and his Greek-named colleagues are brought before the apostles for prayers and laying on of hands (6:6). The evidence of divine approval is multiple: Stephen is described as "full of grace and power" and as performing "great wonders and signs among the people" (6:8). Indeed, his antagonists in their disputes with Stephen "could not withstand the wisdom and Spirit with which he spoke" (6:10). The same kinds of evidence show divine approbation of what Stephen is doing in his *diakonia* as accompanied the work of the apostles. Similarly, when he is facing a martyr's death, he sees the Holy Spirit, the glory of God and the exalted Son of Man (7:55–56). Likewise, Philip is reported as preaching and performing signs, wonders and exorcisms exactly as the apostles do (8:4–8, 12–13). The Spirit guides him and prepares his hearer, the Ethiopian eunuch, precisely as is soon to be done for Peter in relation to the launching of the Gentile mission in the house of Cornelius (Acts 10). The combination of instructions through the Spirit, interpretation of scriptures to confirm what is happening, and the direct activity of the Spirit in moving the messenger are found in both these accounts. The major difference seems to be that in the stories told about the apostles, a central factor is the establishment of precedents and the corporate approval of new tactics or approaches to new audiences. Yet in the stories of Stephen and Philip the beginning of the spread of the gospel in Judaea, Samaria and beyond has already begun. The task of proclamation and the divine approval through the Spirit and wonders are shared by various types of actors in Acts. The policy making is the exclusive prerogative of the apostles, however.

What is involved in *diakonia* is indicated directly throughout Acts. When the process of choosing a successor for Judas is described (1:17), there is mention that the betrayer had been allotted a share "in this ministry" (*diakonia*). Matthias, Judas' successor, is selected to take his place in this *diakonia* and apostleship – thus combining the two terms, although the two roles are not merely merged (1:25). The term is also used in Acts 11:29 with reference to the relief that was sent to the Judaean Christians during a time of famine. The ministry of Paul and his associates in various places and in his report to the Jerusalem community about his activities is linked with the term, *diakonia* (12:25 in Judaea; 20:24 in Greece; in his report in Jerusalem (21:19). Clearly *diakonos* is for the author of Acts not a technical designation of an ecclesiastical office, but the function of *diakonia* – of the word, in preaching and teaching, and in performance of signs and wonders – is a major factor in the outreach of the gospel to the ends of the earth.

1.3 Elders

Unlike *diakonos*, which is not found in Acts, the term elder occurs rather frequently in this book, but any definition of the role of elder or specification of qualifications is lacking. The first mention of elders is in connection with the famine relief effort for the communities in Judaea arranged by the churches in Antioch (11:27–30). Barnabas and Saul are the ones chosen to take the gift "to the elders" in Judaea. Similarly, the delegation sent from Antioch to Jerusalem to settle the dispute over circumcision as a requirement for membership in the new people of God is appointed "to go up to the apostles and the elders about this question" (15:2). Elders participate in the welcome to these visitors from Antioch, along with the church and the apostles (15:4), and elders and apostles assembled to discuss the issue (15:6). It is this three-fold assemblage – church, apostles, elders – which formulates the official position and which appears in the salutation of the letter sent to Antioch (15:22, 23). It is the decision of the apostles and elders that is reported to the churches in Asia Minor (16:4). When Paul returns to Jerusalem for the last time, it is to James and the elders that he makes his report of what God has done among the Gentiles (21:18). Elders are not a feature unique to the

Jerusalem community, however, since Paul and Barnabas appointed elders in every church that they established in their initial journey across Asia Minor (14:23). Nothing more can be inferred from this evidence than that, according to Acts and in keeping with Old Testament tradition, the designation given to respected members of the community whose capacity for decision-making and stability maintenance was respected was "elder".[4] As is the case with *diakonos*, there is in Acts no job description for an elder analogous to that found in the deutero-Paulines (I Tim. 5).

1.4 Episkopos

Unlike the case with *diakonos*, which is not found in Acts, the term *episkopos* does appear, but not as the title for an ecclesiastical office. Cognate terms are also used and some hints are given of what might be called an episcopal function. The process of choosing a successor to Judas (1:15–26) is justified by appealing to passages of scripture, including Ps. 109:8 (LXX) which advises "let another person assume his *episkopen*". In the three other occurrences of this term in the New Testament, only one refers to an ecclesiastical office: I Tim. 3:1. The other two point to the day of divine judgment that is to come (Luke 19:44; I Peter 2:12). The psalm quoted is one of the imprecatory type, calling for judgment on one's enemy, including seizure of the family resources – here identified as *episkope*. The Hebrew term, *pakad*, usually means accumulated wealth, but it can also mean appointed post. The logic of the psalm calls for the former signification, but the LXX rendered it in the latter sense – which fits well the concern of the author of Acts. The implication seems to be that one should equate the role of disciple with that of apostle, and also of *episkopos*. The only passage where the function of overseeing is detailed (20:28–32) is one in which the cognate verb appears rather than either of the nouns mentioned above. In his address to the elders of the Ephesian church (20:17–35) Paul exhorts them to take care about their own manner of life as well as that of the flock in whose charge they have been placed by the Holy Spirit, so that they might "shepherd the church of God". He warns them against fierce opposition from without and serious perversions of the faith from within, which will result in divisions among the people of God. The resources of which he reminds them are God and the word of his grace, which can achieve building of the community and sharing in the inheritance of faith. Although the responsibilities sketched here are specific and essential for the continuity of the church, the designation of *episkopos* seems to be a metaphor of leadership responsibility for the flock of God rather than an ecclesiastical office.

1.5 *Teacher*

As we shall see in our analysis of the functions operative within the community as depicted by Acts, teaching is a major responsibility and a primary means of extending and maintaining its membership. The paradigm for this role is Jesus himself, whose career is epitomized in Acts 1:1 as what he "began to do and teach". That this activity is only the beginning of what God is doing through the apostles emphasizes both continuity with what Jesus launched and expansion far beyond the geographically limited scope of his ministry. References to the teaching activity of the apostles, and especially of Paul, are frequent in Acts. Yet only in 13:1 is their direct mention of the role of teacher – in this case, within the community at Antioch. In their capacity as prophets and teachers there, several of the leaders are instructed through the Spirit to set apart Barnabas and Saul to launch the wider mission to the Gentiles.

1.6 *Prophet*

In Peter's sermon in the portico of Solomon in the temple, Jesus is identified as the promised eschatological prophet whose coming was announced in Deut. 18:15–20. What he will accomplish is in fulfilment of what the other prophets had announced, from Samuel onwards through the history of Israel (Acts 3:17–24). His hearers are acclaimed by him as the children and heirs of those prophets and of the inclusive covenant promised to Abraham which will bring the blessings of God to "all the families of the earth" (3:25–26).

Not only the fulfilment of the prophetic promises but also the exercise of the prophetic function are to be operative within the new community as well. The outpouring of the Spirit on the Day of Pentecost is linked with the prophecy of Joel (3:1) which tells that sons and daughters will prophecy (Acts 2:17). But prophet is also depicted in Acts as a kind of office, as when Judas and Silas are sent to Antioch by the Jerusalem apostles and a mention is made that they "were themselves prophets" (15:22). This identification is repeated in 15:32, where we read that these emissaries from Jerusalem exhorted and strengthened the members of the community in Antioch. When Paul bestows the Spirit on the believers in Ephesus, they speak with tongues and prophecy (19:6). On Paul's final return to Palestine, the four daughters of Philip are reported to have prophesied (21:9), and a prophet, Agabus, visits Paul in Caesarea, warning him of the opposition that awaits him in Jerusalem (21:10). The ecstatic as well as the predictive features of prophecy seem to be assumed in the Acts references to this phenomenon, and the whole of the purpose of God through Jesus is set in the framework of prophetic pronouncement and fulfilment.

2. Terms for Describing the New Community

2.1 Believers

By far the most common and pervasive designation for those who share in the new community is "those who believe". In some cases there is an indication of what was believed – examples include "the word", "in the name", "the Lord Jesus" – but often the term occurs in the absolute sense of "have faith" or "trust" without direct object expressed or implied. At Pentecost, those who "received the word" of Peter and were baptized (2:41) are soon described more succinctly as "all who believed" (2:44). The wide response to the gospel from hearers in the Jerusalem area is repeatedly mentioned in Acts: 'Many who heard the word believed" (4:4); "the multitude of those who believed" (4:32); "More believers were added to the Lord" (5:14). In Samaria, those who believed were baptized, both men and women (8:12), and at Joppa the restoration of Dorcas to life leads many to believe in the Lord (9:42).

The crucial principle of potentially universal inclusion in the new community is articulated by Peter at the house of Cornelius: "Everyone who believes in [Jesus] receives forgiveness of sins through his name" (10:43). A similar basic affirmation is uttered by Paul in the synagogue in Antioch-in-Pisidia when he declares that "everyone that believes" is freed from the obligations that the law of Moses demands but makes no provision for liberation from or for forgiveness (13:39). In accord with the inscrutable purpose of God, scoffers will never believe (13:41). Conversely, "as many as were ordained to eternal life believed" (13:48). It is God who chose Peter to be the first one through whom Gentiles would hear the gospel and believe (15:7).

The response of believing is described in Acts in relationship to individuals as well as to larger groups. When the proconsul in Cyprus sees Paul's punitive miracle against Elymas the magician, he believes (13:12). The jailer in Philippi, together with his entire household believe when Paul tells them that to believe on the Lord Jesus will lead to their being saved (16:31, 34). In Athens, following Paul's address to the Areopagites, some hearers – male and female – join them and believe (17:34). In Corinth, Crispus, the ruler of the synagogue, believed together with his household and many other Corinthians (18:8). Those who believe include both Gentiles – as in Antioch (11:17, 21) – and Jews in Iconium (14:1) and Beroea (17:12), and "certain of the Pharisees" (15:5). In their final interchange in Jerusalem, James tells Paul that there are thousands among the Jews who have believed who still are persuaded that all Christians should observe the law of Moses (21:20), but he goes on to assert the policy agreed upon by the apostles which frees the Gentiles "who believe" from all but a minimal core of legal requirements (21:25). Recalling his program of persecution of the church, he tells how in his mystical encounter with the risen Christ he had confessed that "in every synagogue I beat and imprisoned those who believed in you."

The connotations of "believe" as used in Acts are clarified when there are reports that Paul believes "everything laid down by the law or written in the prophets" (24:14) or when he asks King Agrippa if he believes all that is in the law and the prophets (26:27). Most clearly the import of believing is conveyed when he describes his having explained to the crew of the ship on which he was bound for Rome that an angel had assured him of his arrival and of his standing trial there, and that he then declared, "I trust in God that it will be exactly as I have been told" (27:25). To believe is to rely upon the promise of God, laid down in the scriptures or conveyed through the Holy Spirit or by vision of the divine. Those who share this response to what God has said and done and continues to do are the ones that Acts characterizes as "the believers".

2.2 Brethren

To refer to the covenant community members as "brothers" was not a Christian innovation. Acts shows that this was a general and widely-used way of designating those in the Jewish community from Jerusalem to Rome. In the account of Peter's address in the temple on the day of Pentecost, he speaks to his fellow Jews and God-fearers gathered there as "brethren" (2:29), and they use the same term in their subsequent question to him as to what they should now do in response to this message and the outpouring of the Spirit (2:37). Similarly, Stephen so addresses his hearers when he is on trial before the high priest (7:2). It is Paul's form of address to his hearers in the synagogue at Antioch-in-Pisidia, following the reading of the scriptures (13:15), as well as in his appeal to them to understand what God has done through the death and resurrection of Jesus (13:26, 38). It is the term he uses with reference to the letters he received from the high priest to the Jews of Damascus when he undertook to exterminate the Christian movement there (22:5). It is the way in which the Jews of Rome refer to the Jewish visitors who had come to Rome from Judaea, none of whom had reported anything negative about Paul or the movement (28:21). Thus brotherhood, with all of its male chauvinist connotations, was seen as the appropriate way to designate the covenant people of God as the author of Acts portrays Judaism in this period.

The term is applied from the outset to the Christian community as well, beginning in Jerusalem even before the coming of the Spirit at Pentecost, and numbering "about one hundred and twenty" (1:15). It is "the brethren" who provide safe conduct for Paul to Caesarea after he is threatened for the first time in Jerusalem, and who send him off to Tarsus (9:30). The report of Peter's miraculous release from prison is to be reported to "James and the brethren" (12:17). It is by that designation that they are addressed by James when the formal decision is made about requirements for admission of Gentiles to the church (15:13). This term as a comprehensive label for the church is evident in Acts 15:23 where the letter from Jerusalem to the church in Antioch is prefaced by the words, "The brethren, both the apostles and the elders."

The second half of Acts 15:23 shows that "brethren" was also used for communities in other parts of the empire as well.

Those addressed here are "the brethren who are of the Gentiles in Antioch and Syria and Cilicia." The precedent for this is set earlier in Acts when Peter is accompanied to the house of Cornelius by "some of the brethren from Joppa" (10:23), who were six in number, according to his later report in Jerusalem (11:12). The opposition that Paul and Barnabas encounter in Iconium when large numbers of Jews and Greeks are converted is said to be turned against "the brethren" (14:2). The community in Antioch is so designated with respect to the raising of the issue of legal obligations for Gentile Christians (15:1) and the resolution of the difficulty through the delegation from Jerusalem (15:32–33). It is the "brethren" who commend Paul and Silas to God's grace as they set out on the next phase of the mission to the Gentiles (15:40), an undertaking that will take them to visit "the brethren in every city" (15:36). The term is used with reference to the Christian communities in Lystra and Iconium (16:2), Thessalonica (17:6, 10), Beroea (17:14), Corinth (18:18), Ephesus (18:27), and Ptolemais (21:7). It is also found in the brief accounts of Christian communities in Italy, at Puteoli (28:14) and in Rome itself (28:15). Just as "believer" points to the requirement for admission to the community, so "brethren" indicates the communal, even familial nature of the associations in the new community. Other titles for the community indicate other facets of its common life.

2.3 Ekklesia

The fact that this is not a term peculiar to Christianity is apparent from its occurrence with reference to both Jewish and Christian assemblies: the gathering of the tribes of Israel at Sinai (7:38) and the civic assembly in Ephesus (19:32, 39). With reference to the church as the gathering of Christians, the term *ekklesia* in Acts designates either a specific local congregation or the cluster of churches in a specific region. The first appearance of the term in Acts (5:11) occurs in connection with the punitive miracle that occurred when Ananias and Sapphira cheated by failing to turn over their entire property to the Christian community. When their death is reported, "great fear came upon the whole church" – which presumably is limited to those of the new community in Jerusalem. Soon, however, the preaching of the gospel by the Hellenists and others driven out of "the church in Jerusalem" (8:1) by the persecution has resulted in a church which spreads "throughout all Judaea and Galilee and Samaria" (9:31). The violent attack on the church by Herod Agrippa I described in 12:1ff. seems to have been concentrated on the apostolic leaders who had remained in Jerusalem (8:1). Elsewhere in Acts, "church" refers to local congregations in Jerusalem (11:22, 26; 12:5; 15:4, 22), in Antioch (13:1; 14:27; 15:3), and in Ephesus (20:17).

The churches are described as gathering (14:27)[5] and as appointing delegates to carry messages or perform inspection visits (15:3, 4; 15:22). Among the functionaries in these churches are mentioned prophets and teachers (13:1) and elders (20:17–18). The latter are appointed in each church by Paul and Barnabas (13:23). As we noted, it is the elders who are to be the overseers (*episkopous*) who shepherd the church at Ephesus (20:18, 28). Thus Acts reflects the movement within the community of the first century toward both consciousness of group identity and assignment of responsibility to certain members for various leadership roles.

2.4 Saints

A less frequent term in Acts to describe the community of faith is saints. It occurs only with reference to Paul's oppression of the Christians in Jerusalem and Damascus (9:13; 26:10), and in connection with Peter's visit to those living near the Mediterranean coast at Joppa and Lydda. This is in sharp contrast to the pervasive presence of this term for the church in the letters of Paul.

2.5 Disciples

One of the most frequently occurring designations for the new community in Acts is *mathetai*. Obviously akin to the term for the inner circle of Jesus' followers in the gospel tradition, it appears in Acts as a far broader descriptive indication of members of the communities in both Jewish and predominantly Gentile areas. The growth of the church in Jerusalem is described in 6:1 and 6:7 as the great increase in the number of the disciples. This is the group formally assembled by the twelve apostles to hear the official decree about the division of labor between service of the word and serving tables. It is the disciples who are the targets of the effort of Paul to extirpate what he regarded as a subversive movement (9:1), and it is one of the disciples – Ananias – who leads him to faith in Jesus as the Christ (9:10). In Damascus (9:25), in Jerusalem (9:26), in Joppa (9:38), in Antioch (10:26, 29; 13:52; 14:28), in Lystra (14:20), in Derbe (14:21), in Galatia and Phrygia (18:23), in Ephesus (19:1, 9; 20:1), in Tyre (21:4) and Caesarea (21:16), the Christian community is referred to as disciples.

Their role as disciples includes providing support for the church in Jerusalem (10:29). There is the possibility that attacks from outside the group by "wolves" may take members away from the disciples, as at Ephesus (20:30), while the proclamation of the gospel is what makes disciples (14:21). Indeed, the term may be used for the church as a whole, as in the decree of the apostolic council with its concern to avoid putting the yoke of the law on the neck of the disciples (15:10). The term is used without significant reference to the role of disciples as "learners". Its connotations seem to be rather that of adherent. Perhaps most significant is the mention in 10:26 that disciples in Antioch were first called "Christians" – that is, members of the group who identify themselves, their values and destiny with this Jesus whom they call the Christ.

3. Life-style of the New Community

The fullest account of the earliest Christian community occurs in the Acts description of the impact of the outpouring of the Spirit on the faithful gathered in Jerusalem (2:41–47). The number of members has soared from 120 (1:15) to about 3,000. Their participation in the movement is grounded on their having received the word and accepted baptism. Their ongoing activities within the community include devoting themselves to the instruction which the apostles offered, to fellowship (*koinonia*), to breaking bread and to prayers. That this fellowship is far more than a feeling of togetherness or merely verbal sharing is evident in the details which follow, where we learn that all possessions are pooled, including the selling of the property of each member and depositing the results in the common fund. Any in special need received support from the pooled resources. Their common religious experience – which resembles outwardly the practices of the Pharisees – included daily attendance at the temple and the breaking of bread. It could be debated whether the latter was merely sharing common meals or the celebration of the eucharist in connection with the meal. The answer is probably, "Both." The atmosphere evoked by these common activities is one of happiness, generosity, and praise to God. The response of the populace of Jerusalem as a whole is said to be that they were finding "favor with all the people." The impact was so positive and attractive that daily there were more converts and the number of the community membership was increasing.

A similar picture of the Jerusalem Christian community is offered in Acts 4:32–37. There we hear of a unity of heart and soul, and the detail is repeated that the members placed all their resources in the common fund, and that as a result there were no needy members, since what was required in each case was provided from the group treasury. Houses and lands were sold, and the profits pooled. The daily needs of each member were supplied from this common fund. Among those who joined the group and contributed their possessions was a Levite named Joseph. So important for the identity of the group and its quality of life was the sharing of possessions that a punitive miracle strikes down Ananias and Sapphira when they cheat and hold back some of their resources (5:1–11).

There are three words which succinctly characterize this common life of the early Christian community depicted in Acts: *koinos, koinonia,* and *homothumadon.* The first two are the adjective *koinos* which describes the pooling of resources and the shared experience; the noun *koinonia* which is the condition resulting from this shared existence. The adverb *homothumadon* defines the quality of life of this community. It is first used in Acts in connection with the gathering of the twelve in Jerusalem to await the promised Spirit (1:14). The apostles devote themselves to prayer, in association with "the women and Mary, the mother of Jesus, and with his brothers." There is no indication who the women are, but throughout the Gospel of Luke there are references to women associated with Jesus in his public ministry, as we shall note below. The commonality of life is underscored by the use of this adverb in 2:46 (the description of the post-Pentecost community) and in the corporate prayer reported in 4:23ff., as well as in the vivid scene in the Portico of Solomon, where the group is gathered and where the divine approbation is given through the signs and wonders that the apostles are enabled to perform (5:12–16). The numbers continue to swell, including "multitudes of both men and women" (5:14).

The participation of women in the movement is highlighted

throughout Luke and Acts – a sociological factor which stands in contrast to Judaism and to respectable religious movements in Roman society.[6] In Luke's infancy narratives, women have the dominant roles, in contrast to that of the males who are passive or disbelieving. Both Mary and Elizabeth are referred to as handmaids of the Lord. It is Mary who understands what God is going to do through her son (2:1–20). It is she who is pronounced blessed by Simeon (2:33 and Anna the prophetess (2:36). It is she who understands God's purpose through Jesus (2:51) and whose blessedness Luke pronounces (11:27–28). In his narratives about Jesus Luke alone reports the healing of the widow's son (7:11–17). Luke has moved the story of the woman anointing Jesus from the passion section to the early, formative part of Jesus' ministry (7:36–50). His is the only account of the woman with the spirit of infirmity (13:10–17), and he alone reports the Parable of the Joyous Housewife (15:8–10). Analogous to the support group in Acts is the uniquely Lukan mention of the women in Galilee who provide for Jesus and his followers out of their own means (8:1–3). Significantly, one of them, Joanna, is the wife of an important figure in the royal establishment of Herod Antipas, the tetrarch of Galilee. Similarly, in Luke's post-resurrection scenes, women play a prominent role. What is conveyed in both Luke and Acts, therefore, is a redefined *koinonia*, in which women have a significant share.

Homothumadon is also used in the description of crowds in Samaria who welcome the messengers of the gospel and their message (8:6). It occurs in Acts' characterization of the common mind of the apostles in Jerusalem when the official position is adopted concerning legal requirements for Gentiles admitted to the Christian fold (15:25). Ironically, it is found as well in Acts in the accounts of the rallying of opposition to the gospel and its proclaimers in Jerusalem (7:57), in Tyre (12:20), in Corinth (18:12), and in Ephesus (19:29). Common belief and concerted action are implicit in *omothumadon*, whether for or against the gospel. Yet Christianity is not portrayed in Acts as a mass movement. The characteristic place of meeting of the community is in homes (2:46; 5:42; 8:3; 18:7), although there will be a move to public halls if that is required by the local circumstances, as was the case in Ephesus, where a public hall was hired for the meeting of the local community (19:9). There are repeated references to conversions by households, as in the case of Cornelius (10:2; 11:14), Lydia (16:15), and Crispus in Corinth (18:8). To join the new community is not an isolated, individualistic decision, but a choice of a new mode of group identity: the newly defined and constituted covenant people of God.

4. The Strategy of the New Community

4.1 Proclamation

The primary role of the members of the new community is proclamation. At the end of the Gospel of Luke, the risen Jesus commissions the disciples to preach "repentance and forgiveness of sins . . . in his name" to all nations (24:47). As witnesses of his life and work, and now as those who have encountered him raised from the dead, they are specially prepared to bear this testimony, "beginning from Jerusalem". The enabling and confirming power of the Spirit is soon to be poured out on them as they launch this world-encompassing enterprise (24:48).

Beginning with Peter's address to the throngs on the day of Pentecost (Acts 2:14–36), that is the primary strategy of the apostles to fulfil their divinely-assigned task. The same tactic is employed in his speech in Solomon's Portico (3:11–26). The official opposition arises in direct response to this "proclaiming in Jesus the resurrection from the dead" (4:2). In spite of these official injunctions, the apostles continue to give "their testimony to the resurrection of the Lord Jesus" (4:33) and to bear witness to God's having exalted Jesus at his right hand as Leader and Savior (5:30–31). Those scattered as a result of the persecution of the Christians in which Saul participated "went about preaching the word", including proclaiming Christ to the Samaritans (8:4–5). Immediately upon his conversion, Paul preaches Jesus to those in the synagogues of Damascus (9:20). In his address to the household of Cornelius, Peter notes his and the other apostles' role as witness of what Jesus did and of his resurrection, and concludes with the commission Jesus had given them "to preach to the people, and to testify that he is the one ordained by God to be the judge of the living and the dead" (10:42). The apostles' testimony is confirmed by the witness of the prophets to him (10:42).

The substance of Paul's witness is epitomized by the Jewish

exorcists in Ephesus as "Jesus whom Paul preaches" (19:13). Similarly, in his farewell to the representatives of the Ephesian church who meet him as he is en route to Jerusalem for the last time, he summarizes the work that he carried out in his mission as "preaching the kingdom" (20:25). And during his period under house arrest in Rome, Acts reports him as "preaching the kingdom of God" (28:31). Proclamation of the gospel is the essential point of beginning of the mission to the world to which God calls the apostles in the account in Acts.

4.2 Instruction

The model for the basic activity appropriate to the members of the community is Jesus, according to the opening verse of Acts. The Gospel of Luke, or "the first book", dealt with "all that Jesus began to do and teach". The activity of the apostles that draws down the wrath of high priest and other religious leaders is that the followers of Jesus are now "teaching the people" (4:2), and doing so in his name (4:18). Following the miraculous release of the apostles from prison (5:17–21), the angel of the Lord told them to "stand in the temple and speak to the people all the words of this life" – an activity which is described as teaching, and for which they were so eager that they began their public instructional activity at dawn. The officers who recognize them as escapees and the officials who sent them to prison are one in describing the activity of the apostles as teaching the people in the name of Jesus (5:25, 28). In spite of the persecutions, imprisonment and official prohibitions they spend every day in the temple and in homes in ceaseless "teaching and preaching Jesus as the Christ" (5:42). It is noteworthy that, while teaching is joined with preaching in these summary statements, the primary emphasis is on teaching. In these earlier chapters of Acts, teaching is a public activity with what might be called evangelistic intentions, rather than instruction offered for the already committed within the community.

On-going instruction is an important feature of these communities as the author of Acts portrays them, however. When Saul was brought from Tarsus to Antioch by Barnabas, his role was to meet with the members of the church, which he did over the course of a year, offering instruction to "a large company of people" (11:25). Similarly, on their return from the council with the apostles in Jerusalem (Acts 15), Paul and

Barnabas remain in Antioch teaching and preaching the word
of the Lord, along with "many others" – i.e., presumably other
teachers. In Corinth, Paul is reported as remaining there for a
year and a half "teaching the word of God among them"
(18:11). Another vivid example of the instructional program of
the church is Apollos, who was powerful in handling the
scriptures and had been instructed in the way of the Lord. He
was able to tell and teach "accurately the things concerning
Jesus", including the tradition about John the Baptist and
his rite, but needed more accurate information and insights
concerning "the way of the Lord". These were provided him
by Priscilla and Aquila (18:24–27). It is wholly in keeping with
the overall viewpoint of Acts that the final portrait of Paul,
awaiting trial in Rome, represents him as not only "preaching
the kingdom of God" but also "teaching about the Lord Jesus
quite openly" (28:31). This is literally and figuratively the final
note with which Acts brings to a close his vivid account of the
apostolic mission and its results.

4.3 Apologetics

The apostles and Paul in Acts are portrayed as engaging in
three different tactics in order to get their message about Jesus
through persuasively and appropriately to three different
audiences. For Jewish and Jewish-oriented Gentile hearers,
the approach is the exposition of the scriptures. At every
important stage in the Acts narrative, beginning with the
Pentecost scene and continuing through to the stage where
the primary audiences are those on the periphery of Judaism
(God-fearers, Samaritans, and Ethiopians), the basic argument
that Jesus is the Christ derives from the Christian interpretation
of the law and the prophets. Not only is direct fulfilment
claimed, but there are basic precedents set in the history of
Israel which find their full and renewed meaning in the epoch
of Jesus.

For Gentile hearers, there is an approach which points
to certain detailed correspondences between what Graeco-
Roman philosophers have said and what God is saying and
doing through Jesus. The most famous of these is, of course,
Paul's address to the Areopagites (Acts 17). But in his explanation to the pagans in Lystra who want to identify him and
Barnabas as Hermes and Zeus he gives utterance to ideas about
the creation and providential care of the universe that are

commonplaces of Stoic philosophy even while being compatible with certain strands in the scriptures as well (14:15–18). It is understandable why the crowds acclaim them as gods in human form, so firm is the harmony between the early Christian and the philosophical views as set forth here in Acts. It is easy to see how this tactic was developed by the fathers of the church in the second century, building on the precedents of hellenistic Jewish thinkers like the author of IV Maccabbees and Philo of Alexandria. Indeed, there is precedent for the synthesis of Stoic and Christian views in the letters of Paul.[7]

The third audience addressed in Acts is Roman, and specifically the political authorities. In the trial scenes which bring the book to a close, Paul is repeatedly exonerated by the regional Roman officials. Yet his appeal to the supreme adjudicating authority of the emperor is sustained. His case is set forth effectively in Acts 28:17–18. Taken captive by the religious authorities, he was turned over to the political powers of Rome. They had found him innocent of any violation of Roman law and were ready to set him free. Pressed by the Jewish officials, the Romans had agreed as a kind of compromise to allow Paul to exercise his citizenship privilege and to make his appeal directly to Caesar. Under military guard on his arrival in Rome (28:16), he continues in that status even while living in his own rented quarters over a period of two years (28:30). His controversies are entirely with Jews, who do not accept his claims about Jesus or his interpretations of the Jewish scriptures. There is no hint of subversion on the part of Paul, and no trace of a political charge that could be sustained against him.

This dimension of the Acts narrative, with its implicit and explicit denial that Paul is in any sense a threat to the Roman order, was a highly important feature of the writing at the time it was produced: around the end of the first century CE or the beginning of the second. Although the evidence is not unambiguous, it seems probable that there was in Rome some action against the Christians under Domitian. The report in Dio Cassius' *Roman History* (67:14) about Domitian's having executed Flavius Clemens and Flavia Damitilla, members of the imperial family, on the charge of atheism as a result of their having drifted in Jewish ways, may point to their having converted to Christianity. This confusion of Judaism and Christianity appears in another ancient Roman historian,

Suetonius, who reports in his *Lives of the Twelve Caesars* that the emperor Claudius (reigned 41–54 CE) expelled all Jews from Rome when their community was split and in conflict that arose "at the instigation of Chrestos" – which is almost certainly a mistaken reference to Christos. The arrival in Rome of the message about Jesus as Messiah – or Christos – in the late forties would have been violently disruptive to the Jewish community there. This incident is mentioned in Acts 18:1–2, since that was what had brought Aquila and Priscilla from Rome to Corinth. By the time Paul wrote his letter to the Romans, they were back in Rome, as Paul's greetings to them shows (Rom. 16:3). Nero's persecution of the Christians in Rome is attested in the Roman historian Tacitus (*Annals* 15.44), although he treats it as an isolated incident and as a tactic of Nero to cover up his own involvement in the burning of Rome. For certain, the issue of how to treat the Christians who refused to honor the emperor as divine had come to a head in the reign of Trajan (98–117), as is shown in the famous correspondence between him and Pliny, the governor of the Asian province of Bithynia,[8] in which Christians are not to be sought out, but if brought before the Roman authorities are to be forced to offer the sacrifices on penalty of death. There is no mistaking that this issue of the official Roman response to the emergent Christian movement was coming into focus in the last decades of the first century. What response were the Christians to make? The author of Acts gives one clear answer: they are not violators of Roman law or fomentors of nationalistic revolt. The fundamental issues for the Christians are between them and Jewish interpreters of the scriptural traditions on the question of participation in the covenant people of God. There is no aggression on their part toward Rome, and on the basis of problems that have come to the attention of the Roman officials, the uniform judgment of the Romans has been that the Christians are not violators of or threats to the empire. Acts subtly, but consistently and effectively, makes this crucial point.

The final scene in Acts calls emphatic attention to the conviction that what is happening and what is yet to happen in the outreach of the gospel are manifestations of God's rule in the world. Paul is seen as expounding the scriptures from morning to night in order to persuade his Jewish hearers from the law and prophets that Jesus is God's agent for the renewal

of his people and for the accomplishment of God's rule in the
creation (= "the kingdom of God"). Even the resistance of his
hearers to the message is seen to be in accord with scripture
(28:25–27 = Isa. 6:9–10). Their opposition does not thwart
God's saving purpose, but contributes instead to its going out
now to the wider Gentile audience, and "they *will* listen"
(28:28). It is this combination of God's exercising his rule in
the world and the instruction about Jesus as God's Messiah
which are the essence of Paul's work in Rome and of the book
of Acts as a whole. It is this conviction which provides the
motivation for the work of proclamation, instruction and
apologetics, and it is also seen as the source of power by which
this world-wide task is in process of being accomplished.

6

Witnesses to the Ends of the Earth

1. The Ground and Content of the Witness

Although Acts obviously offers an account of the origins and of the church and the initial stages of its spread from Jerusalem to Rome, it is by no means intended as primarily an historical record. The book recounts the steps by which the covenant community was redefined from its original basis in ethnic Israel to its wider group understanding as potentially universal. Acts also insists on the continuities between the promises of God recorded in the law and the prophets and the fulfilment which is seen to have occurred through Jesus and the apostles. But the major aim of the author is to challenge his readers in the present by informing them about the past, not merely to present an archive of Christian origins.

In making his case for what God has begun to do through Jesus and the apostles, Acts points to the corroborative significance that God has provided for this redefinition of the covenant people by his direct action in human history and in the personal experience of the chief actors. This is discernible, Acts declares, through the work of the Holy Spirit, as well as through the transformation and renewal of those who have participated in this work of God through Jesus. Preeminently it is evident in that God has raised Jesus from the dead, and that resurrection is an event attested by multiple witnesses rather than a private experience of a solitary mystic. Further confirmation of the reliability of these claims of renewal comes from the evidence that so many people who were on the fringe of Israel or far beyond its covenantal boundaries now see themselves as part of, and publicly affirm their participation in this new people of God.

Acts also offers assurance that suffering and even death are not signs of divine abandonment nor are they outside the purpose of God. Rather, they are both human experiences which are necessary stages in the fulfilment of God's plan for his people, phases through which some must pass in order that the divine plan for them and for God's people might be fulfilled. Evidence that God has triumphed over suffering and death is dramatically available in the experience of the risen Christ that has been granted to the chosen witnesses: the apostles. Beyond that assurance of God's vindication of the suffering, martyred Jesus is the vision of him exalted at God's right hand, where he is the agent and guarantor of the ultimate triumph of God's redemptive purpose for the whole world. Yet this hope rests not only on the past event of the resurrection of Jesus and the future hope of final victory over the powers of evil, not only in the memory of Jesus in the past and the visions of his present exaltation, but also in the immediate and repeated evidence of God's ongoing presence and action through his people by means of the Spirit at work in their midst. These insights and convictions are not an abstract theological system to be affirmed, but the ground of a task to which God calls his new people: the witness to be borne to the ends of the earth.

2. The Call of the Witnesses

The closing lines of Luke's gospel assert explicitly the unique and essential role of Jesus' disciples as witnesses to "these things" which have been recounted throughout the gospel (Luke 24:48). There is a promise of "power from on high", and there has been an instruction that the message of forgiveness "should be preached in his name to all nations", but for the present they are to remain in Jerusalem as the center and base for all that God has begun to do through Jesus for the renewal of his people. The scope of this challenge is described even more dramatically in Acts 1:8. Following the instructions and the proofs of his resurrection over a period of forty days,[1] the formation of the new community is ready to be launched. In these early sermons and speeches, Peter as spokesman for the apostolic circle repeatedly notes that he and his colleagues have witnessed that God raised Jesus from the dead (2:32; 3:15; 5:32), and the narrator of Acts makes the same assertion (4:33).

In his address to the household of Cornelius, Peter expands the scope of his witness to include all that Jesus did in Judaea and Jerusalem (10:39) in addition to his testimony about the resurrection of Jesus (10:40). These claims are further supported by the witness of the prophets, he asserts (10:42), and as Paul later affirms (26:22). Similarly, the appearance of the risen Jesus to the apostles is said by Paul to have qualified them to become "witnesses to the people" (13:31).

As Paul recounts his own experience of conversion and call, he quotes Ananias as having asserted that "the God of our fathers appointed you to know his will, to see the Righteous One and to hear a voice from his mouth; for you will be a witness for him to all men concerning what you have seen and heard" (22:14–15). The same point is made in his address to King Agrippa in 26:16–18: Jesus appeared to Paul in order for him to become a witness to the Gentiles, to whom he has been sent so that they might receive forgiveness and "a place among those who are sanctified by faith in [Christ]". His ability to bear witness to the gospel he received "from the Lord Jesus" (20:24). The ground of his witness is this personal encounter with Jesus, but more specifically with the Jesus whom God has raised from the dead. Essential for the overall aim of Acts is the assurance given to Paul subsequently by "the Lord" that the testimony to Jesus offered in Jerusalem will be repeated by him in Rome itself (23:11). The fulfilment of this promise of witness in its diversity of connotations and locations is effectively epitomized in Acts 28:23, where Paul is said to have expounded the gospel from morning to evening to the Jewish community in Rome, "bearing witness to the Kingdom of God and trying to convince them about Jesus both from the law of Moses and from the prophets." Essential to the witness are the scriptural, prophetic antecedents, which point not only positively to Jesus as the subject of that witness, but also negatively to the rejection of the gospel concerning him by Jews. Most importantly for Acts, the witness of scripture includes as well the reception of that message in faith by many Gentiles (28:25–28).

3. The Prototype of the Witnesses in Acts

The designation of the witnesses in Acts is not a phenomenon invented by the author, but builds rather on a long tradition in the Jewish scriptures. The testimony offered by the witness in this tradition is based on first-hand encounter between God and the individual involved, which results in the latter being commissioned by God to perform a crucial role in relation to the people of God. B.J. Hubbard, in a study of the literary form of Jesus' commissioning of the disciples in Matt. 28:16–20, showed that the basic pattern of this account corresponds to the reports of the commissioning of patriarchs and prophets in the Hebrew Bible.[2] Hubbard finds a common tradition to lie behind Matthew, Luke and John[3] in which these same features are evident. (1) Introduction, in which there are brief indications of the time, place and circumstances in which the encounter occurred: (2) Confrontation, in which the deity or his agent comes to address the individual who is to be commissioned; (3) Reaction, in which the one encountered expresses fear or a sense of unworthiness; (4) Commission, in which the specifics of the task or message to be communicated are given; (5) Protest, in which the person addressed claims he is not qualified for the role; (6) Reassurance, in which the commissioner reaffirms the assignment; (7) Conclusion, rounding off the story with a statement about the assignment that is now being undertaken. Not each of these features is represented in each of the scriptural examples adduced, but the basic pattern prevails.[4] The persons commissioned include men and women, patriarchs and leaders of Israel, a law-giver and prophets, and an unnamed future figure (servant of Yahweh). Hubbard observes that through this experience these people were "summoned . . . to participate in events which shaped the people's destiny".[5] The function of these accounts could be made even more specific, however. What is at stake in each case is that the existence of the community as the people of God is about to undergo a transformation. In the earlier stories, the community is in process of formation; in the latter, it is a promise of renewal through the divinely chosen instrument who has been summoned and challenged by God.

Hubbard proceeded to show how this pattern of commissioning is present in what he regards as the original narrative which underlies the encounter of the risen Jesus with the disciples in Matthew, Luke and John:

Confrontation: Jesus appeared to the eleven.
Reaction: Some were glad; some disbelieved.

Commissioning: They are told to preach to all nations, and to baptize in his name for the forgiveness of sins.
Reassurance: The promise of the Holy Spirit.[6]

In a more recent study, Hubbard has refined this analysis and applied it to the commissioning materials in both Luke and Acts.[7] As is the case with the Old Testament examples, not all the formal features are represented in each instance. But in all 25 of the Luke–Acts occurrences of this phenomenon, there are present an Introduction, Confrontation; Commissioning, Reassurance, and in all but two cases there are Conclusions. Analysis of a representative selection of these commissioning passages in Acts (in addition to the final such scene from Luke) demonstrates the three-fold dimension of witness in Acts: (1) the link between what is written in the law and the prophets and what God is doing through Jesus; (2) the summons of those who are to be the bearers of the good news in word and action; (3) the resultant reconstitution of God's people in response to this testimony.

4. The Commissioning of the Witnesses in Acts

In Luke 24:36–53 Jesus appears to the eleven in Jerusalem. They are frightened and think they are seeing a ghost, but he seeks to reassure them by showing them his hands and feet, by inviting them to handle him, and by sharing food with them. The scriptural witness is then appealed to when he points out to them "everything" written about him in all three divisions of the Jewish canon (24:44), where not only the suffering and resurrection of the Messiah are written, but also the forgiveness of sins which is to be preached in his name *to all nations*, beginning from Jerusalem (24:45–47). To carry out this new role to a new audience, his followers will be given power which he will send them from his place of exaltation "on high". There is a new appropriation of the scriptural witness; there are new events to be attested by these apostolic witnesses: resurrection, ascension and outpouring of the Spirit of God; and there is a new potential audience for this new message: all the nations of the world.

The same features are present in the story of Jesus' meeting with the apostles just prior to his ascension (Acts 1:1–14). The setting is described with reference to the repeated appearances of the risen Lord and the proofs of his resurrection over the period of forty days. Their initial response is to interpret his message about the kingdom of God as the restoration of the Israelite monarchy (1:6), which leads into the commissioning of the apostles to be witnesses to him from Judaea and its neighboring province, Samaria, to the end of the earth. The new factor, in addition to the geographical scope of their testimony, is to be the gift of the Spirit, which Peter's address perceives to be explicitly the fulfilment of the scriptural promise to Joel (2:16). The reassurance that these promises will be fulfilled is given in the taking up of Jesus into the presence of God (1:9–11), as the two men in white robes testify to them. The redefining of covenantal participation is dramatically represented by the world-wide representation at Jerusalem on Pentecost and by the miracle of translation/comprehension which occurs when the Spirit is poured out.

In Acts 8:26–30, Philip is instructed by an angel to seek the Ethiopian inquirer on the road from Jerusalem to Gaza. Each step of the meeting is guided by the Spirit of God. The interpretation of the prophetic scripture leads Philip to tell this seeker "the good news about Jesus". That the eunuch is a non-Israelite trying to discover and understand the purpose of the God of Israel makes the more dramatic the positive response to his question, "What is to prevent my being baptized?" The answer traditionally would have been elaborate and ponderous, involving his ethnic origin, his physical condition, his social involvements. But all the traditional objections to covenantal participation are swept aside in light of his seeking faith in response to Philip's scripture-based witness about Jesus (8:35).

The account in Acts of the conversion of Paul is in two stages: the appearance of the risen Lord to Paul (9:1–9), and the explanation to Paul by Ananias of the significance of that experience (9:10–19). The message Paul hears in his vision of the Lord concerns only his having persecuted Jesus, but initially no explanation follows as to how Paul is to respond to this challenge. Then the disciple Ananias is also encountered in Damascus by the Lord and charged to bear a message to Paul. The response feature of the commissioning model is evident when Ananias protests that this person to whom he is to speak has done such evil to "the saints". The next stage of the commissioning – a further explanation from the Lord –

informs him that Paul "is a chosen instrument of mine to carry my name before the Gentiles and kings and the sons of Israel" (9:15). What is going to happen through Paul is the further extension of activity in behalf of the gospel and broadened participation in the community of faith. After a few days with the disciples in Damascus, Paul's witness to Jesus as Son of God begins "immediately" in the local Jewish meetings (9:19–20). The full launching of the mission to the Gentiles is described in Acts 13, an account which culminates in the pronouncement of Paul to the Jewish antagonists in Pisidian Antioch: the word of God was spoken first to Jews, who have rejected it and the eternal life which it makes possible; now he and Barnabas are turning to the Gentiles. Here (13:47) as justification for the expansion of the scope of his witness, Paul appeals to scripture, which is here quoted as what "the Lord has commanded us": "I have set you to be a light for the Gentiles, that you may bring salvation to the uttermost parts of the earth" (Isa. 49:6).

Precedent for this outreach to Gentiles has already been set in the Acts account (as we have noted) by the commissioning of Peter to go to the household of Cornelius with the gospel (10:9–23). Preparation for the commissioning of Peter has already taken place in the vision of an angel of God that appeared to Cornelius (10:1–8). Peter's call by God to a new role – messenger of the gospel to Gentiles – is described as occurring in a setting which is a model of Jewish piety. He is at prayer on the rooftop at the sixth hour (noon) – perhaps an evidence of extra piety, since the prescribed times of prayer were morning and evening. Further evidence of his piety is provided when, in spite of his hunger, he refuses to eat any of the food lowered down from heaven, because it contained all kinds of ritually unclean items. Then occurs the radical declaration of the heavenly voice: "What God has cleansed, you must not call common". To emphasize this crucial point, the proffering of the food and the instruction to partake of it, as well as the instruction about what God has cleansed, happen three times. The import of this and the evidence that the message got through to Peter are offered in his subsequent meeting with Cornelius and in his address to the latter's household. To Cornelius Peter expresses the contrast between the law forbidding Jews to associate with or to visit non-Israelites and God's instruction that he is to call no human being unclean or common (10:28). To the hearers within the house of Cornelius he lays down as a basic principle that God shows no ethnic or national partiality, but that he accepts those in any nation who fear him and do what is right (10:34–35). This statement is a mosaic of scriptural texts and phrases, including Deut. 10:17; Ps. 15:2; Sirach 35:12. His address ends with the words central to our theme: 'To [Jesus as God's agent] all the prophets bear witness that everyone who believes in him receives forgiveness of sins through his name" (10:43).

A major new stage in Paul's gospel witness is prepared for through another commissioning experience described in Acts 16:8–10. The messenger in the vision is human, not God or Jesus or an angel. But the message conveyed involves an important change in locus for the proclamation of the gospel: from the lands contiguous to Palestine to the mainland of Europe, the center of the Gentile culture and political power. The significance of the vision is given in Paul's conclusion that the call to preach there was from God. Confirmation of this inference is provided by the conversion of Lydia and the Philippian jailer, but by such dramatic accompaniments of these religious experiences as the expulsion of a demon from a soothsayer (16:16–18) and the earthquake which loosens the bonds of the imprisoned apostolic witnesses at the very moment when they are singing hymns and praying (16:25–26).

The series of trials and hearings to which Paul is subjected on his return to Palestine provide the author of Acts opportunities to retell the story of his initial commissioning, and to do so by introducing details not offered in the earlier account. Appropriate continuity with the traditions of Israel is included in the account in 22:6–16, in that the one who explains to Paul the meaning of his encounter with the risen Christ is Ananias, who is described as "a devout man according to the law, well spoken of by all the Jews who lived [in Damascus]" (22:12). Ananias tells Paul that the one who is appointing him to his role as messenger of the gospel is "the end of our fathers" (22:14). The specific goal of his mission is expressed by Christ: "I will send you far away among the Gentiles." It is not only that he is to preach the gospel to non-Israelites, but he is to do so over a wide geographical span.

Other important dimensions of Paul's role as witness are set out in the second of these official reports by him of his conversion (26:12–20). The root of the gospel in the traditions of Israel is clearly implied when the voice of Jesus addresses Paul "in the Hebrew language". The testimony Paul is to bear is based on his own direct experience, in the past, present and future: "I have appeared to you for this purpose, to appoint you as an agent and witness concerning the things which you have seen and in which I shall be seen by you." Acts portrays Paul as having seen Jesus risen from the dead, as having been called by him and repeatedly encountering Jesus in his ongoing role as witness to Christ. His assignment is far more than merely to report verbally what he has seen, important though that is. He has an essential role to fulfil as the God's agent – voluntary but fully empowered and authorized[8] – and witness to the powers and purpose of the one who commissioned him. As we have seen to be characteristic of Acts, the phrasing of this commission is a mosaic of scriptural allusions. The promise of deliverance recalls the assurance to Jeremiah (Jer. 1:8) that God will preserve him as he fulfils his prophetic role and will empower him in relation to the fulfilment of God's purpose among the nations of the world. The same hope of deliverance from the nations is expressed in the words of David in the account in II Chronicles 16 of the dedication of the temple. The prayer ends with the words, "Deliver us, O God of our salvation, and gather and save us from among the nations, that we may give thanks to thy holy name, and glory in thy praise. Blessed be the Lord God of Israel . . . " (16:35–36). But instead of deliverance *from* the nations in the sense of escaping from them or judgment being brought upon them, the other scriptural allusion in Acts 26:18 makes precisely the opposite point: that the nations may turn from darkness to light. This is a reference to Isa. 42:6–7, in which Yahweh announces to the prophet and his community, "I have established you as a light for the peoples [of the earth], a lamp to the nations, to open the eyes that are blind to bring out the prisoners from the dungeon, from the prison those who sit in darkness". Other relevant texts from Isaiah include 35:5 and 61:1 (LXX). These are the "new things" which Yahweh now declares through the prophet (Isa. 42:9). The result of the testimony of word and deed which Paul is called to perform will be that the Gentiles may receive forgiveness *and a place among those who are sanctified in me* (Acts 26:18). The result of this witness is that those previously excluded now find a welcome place within the community of God's new people.

The final commissioning scene reported or described in Acts is that of Paul on the way to Rome (27:21–26). In the midst of the protracted storm at sea Paul reports that there had appeared to him that night "an angel of the God to whom I belong and whom I worship." This deity is not a theological innovation, but the God of the tradition of Israel in which Paul was reared and with which he continues to identify. What is radical about the message from God, however, is that Paul is given assurance that he would stand trial before Caesar, and thus that he and all those on the ship would be preserved from death at sea. He then expresses confidence in God "that it will be exactly as I have been told." Paul's word from God is conveyed to Gentile hearers who share with him the peril of the voyage, but it also gives him assurance that his witness will be heard in the ultimate center of Gentile culture and power: the imperial presence itself.

5. The Authority of the Witness

By way of summary, we may note the factors which lend authority to the testimony of the apostles and Paul. The ground of their claims about Jesus and the new community which God is bringing into being through him is the scriptures: the law, the prophets and the writings. That Jesus is indeed the agent of God is confirmed by the signs and wonders which he performed during the days of his ministry. This is epitomized in the Q saying used by Luke in his gospel (11:20). "If it is by the finger of God that I cast out demons, then the kingdom of God has come upon you." It is significant that the phrase, "finger of God", is used in Ex. 8:19 by Gentile magicians who recognize that the signs and wonders that are preparing for the deliverance of God's people from bondage and their move from enslavement in Egypt to a new beginning as the covenant community in the land of promise are being performed by a god not their own or accessible to their magical arts. In face of the charge that he is performing his exorcisms and signs through a league with Satan, Jesus makes this claim to be God's agent of freedom and renewal of his people.

The two primary grounds for confirming the apostolic witness are the experience of the apostles in having seen Jesus risen from the dead, and the evidence of the Holy Spirit of God at work in their midst and in the lives of the new believers.

But in addition, they are enabled to perform signs and wonders in the name of Jesus, including healings and exorcisms. Equally dramatic evidence in support of their testimony concerning Jesus and God's purpose through him is offered by the actions of God among and through the community or in their behalf. These include punitive miracles, miraculous deliverance from prison, attackers, storms, and deadly animals. The ultimate proof of the claims made in the name of Jesus is the conversion of Gentiles in huge numbers to the belief in Jesus as God's agent to establish and empower the new covenant community. As we have seen, the Acts narratives traces that movement across religious, geographical, ethnic, ritual, intellectual and social boundaries imposed by human perspectives and standards.

The import of this multifold view of witness is articulated in the story in Acts 28:23–28. The Jews in Rome come on an appointed day in great numbers to hear Paul's message. He testified (*diamarturomenos*) throughout the day to them about the kingdom of God in order to convince them about Jesus "from the law of Moses and from the prophets." Some believe, but even the rejection of this witness from scripture is itself represented in Acts as the fulfilment of Isaiah 6:9–10, which is quoted in full. Using a verb that is cognate to the noun, *apostolos*, Acts quotes Paul as saying that "God's salvation has been sent (*apestale*) [i.e., by God] to the Gentiles: they will listen."

6. The Locus of the Witness and the Witnesses

Where is the witness to be made? Initially in Acts, the witness to Jesus as God's agent of covenant renewal is made in Jewish contexts: the temple and synagogues. Even though Paul seems at 13:46 to be turning from testimony to Israel toward witnessing to Gentiles, the Acts narrative reports him and his associates as testifying consistently to Jews,[9] down to the narrative just examined concerning the coming of the Jews to see Paul in Rome. The Acts narratives we have examined show him preaching the gospel in centers of pagan culture and religion, such as the Temple of Artemis in Ephesus and the Areopagus in Athens. More is involved than mere locale: he takes on the issues with these religions. In other settings he exploits the links between the gospel and pagan philosophy or religion in order to point out similarities even while affirming the uniqueness of Christ and the gospel. In Rome, he is prepared to bear his witness before Caesar. Acts is careful to show that Paul and the apostles never engage in civil disobedience, to say nothing of insurrection. At the same time, they stand true to their testimony and refuse to capitulate to pressures to conform to legal pronouncements which would hinder their proclamation of the gospel. Across the entire spectrum of culture, Jewish and Gentile, the witness to Christ and his people is made, bravely and with remarkable skill and insight.

The context of the witness is the new covenant community. It is pictured throughout Acts as growing numerically, in a series of summary-type statements.[10] In 2:41 there are about 3000 in Jerusalem, and the Lord adds daily to their number (2:47). In 6:7, the numbers are multiplied greatly as the community extends into Samaria; in 9:31 the increase is said to be throughout Judaea, Galilee and Samaria, as it is again in 12:24. The Gentile growth is first mentioned in 11:21, 24, where at Antioch "great numbers believed in the Lord" and a large company was added. In 16:5, the numbers in the churches of Asia Minor are reported as increasing daily, and Ephesus the word of God is said to have "prevailed mightily" (19:20). We have seen in the details of our analysis of Acts the mutual support, the shared resources of funds, the common experience of the power of the Spirit that characterizes the church as it is pictured in Acts.

We have also noted the astonishing results of this witness begun in Jerusalem and now being made in Rome itself. But Rome is not the end of the story, even though it is the literary conclusion of Acts. Suggestions that the author intended to write a third volume are pure conjecture and seem contrary to the intent of Acts. The aim of Acts is to show what the resources of the witnessing community are: the power and purpose of God; the birth, life, ministry, death, resurrection and exaltation of Jesus; the outpouring of the Spirit to enable God's people to fulfil their task as witnesses; the scriptures which are the ground of the promises that are being fulfilled through Jesus and the gospel as it is being proclaimed; the strategies that may be employed in order to get the gospel through to potential hearers from a variety of religious and cultural contexts; the mutually supportive community with its range of responsibilities and competences. Above all, the open nature of the new community excludes no one on the basis of present condition, but is open across all humanly-established boundaries.

The world is open. God is in control, and has provided the message and the means to communicate it. The inclusiveness of the new community has been demonstrated in principle, but not yet fully achieved. Paul is the paradigm for the Christian witness (28:30–31): he welcomes all who come to him, regardless of background or condition. He preaches about the kingdom of God and about the Lord Jesus Christ. And he does this "quite openly and unhindered." The important unfinished business in this situation is for the witness of the new community to press forward. Still to be accomplished in the contemporary life of the church is the divine intention revealed to Paul and Barnabas at Pisidian Antioch, midway through the narrative of Acts (13:47): 'I have set you to be a light for the Gentiles, that you may bring salvation to the uttermost parts of the earth."

Notes

1. Perspectives on the Study of Acts

1. The sketch offered here of some major motifs in the study of Acts is not intended as a survey of scholarly studies of Luke-Acts. Useful analyses of these writings include, C.K. Barrett, *Luke the Historian in Recent Study*, London, Epworth Press 1961; W.W. Gasque, *A History of the Criticism of the Acts of the Apostles*, Grand Rapids, Eerdmans 1975; I.H. Marshall, *Luke: Historian and Theologian*, Grand Rapids, Zondervan and Exeter, Paternoster 1970; Eduard Schweizer, *Luke: A Challenge to Present Theology*, Atlanta, John Knox and London, SPCK 1982; F. Bovon, *Luke the Theologian: 33 Years of Research (1950–83)*, Pittsburgh, Pickwick 1987. Full bibliographies include Watson F. Mills, *A Bibliography of the Periodical Literature on the Acts of the Apostles*, Leiden, Brill 19XX; A.J. and M.B. Mattill, *A Classified Bibliography of Literature of the Acts of the Apostles*, Leiden, Brill 1966.

2. In *Das Christentum*, Tübingen 1853, vi–viii. Quoted in P.C. Hodgson, *The Formation of Historical Theology: A Study of F.C. Baur*, New York, Harper 1966, 161.

3. In F.C. Baur, "Über den Ursprung des Episcopats in der christlichen Kirche," Tübingen Zeitschrift für Theologie 3, 1838, translated in W.G. Kümmel, *The New Testament: The History of the Investigation of Its Problems*, trans. S.M. Gilmour and H.C. Kee, Nashville, Abingdon and London, SCM Press 1974, 128–30.

4. Baur, *Paulus, der Apostel Jesu Christi. Ein Beitrag zu einen Kristichen Geschichte des Christentums*, Stuttgart 1845. Quoted from Kümmel, *The New Testament*, 135.

5. Adolf Jülicher, *Einleitung in das Neue Testament*, Freiburg and Leipzig 1894, 436–41.

6. F.J. Foakes-Jackson and H. Lake, *The Beginnings of Christianity*, London, Macmillan 1920–33 (reprinted Grand Rapids, Baker 1965). Cadbury's own substantive studies of literary and historical evidence contemporary with Acts include, *The Making of Luke-Acts*, London, SPCK 1961 (reprint of the 1927 edition), and *The Book of Acts in History*, New York, Harper 1955. His 1920 study, *The Style and Literary Method of Luke* has also been reprinted (New York, Kraus 1969).

7. From the preface to Vol.1 of Foakes-Jackson and K. Lake, *The Beginnings of Christianity, Part I: The Acts of the Apostles*, vii.

8. Martin Dibelius, *Studies in the Acts of the Apostles*, London, SCM Press 1956.

9. Dibelius, *Studies in Acts*, 134, 214.

10. Tübingen, 1954. English translation by G. Buswell, New York, Harper & Row, London, Faber & Faber 1960. The translated title would be "The Mid-point of Time".

11. Ernest Haenchen, *The Acts of the Apostles*, 14th German edition of 1965 trans. R.McL. Wilson et al., Philadelphia, Westminster and Oxford, Blackwell 1971, 90–102.

12. Haenchen, *Acts*, 112–15.

13. Festschrift for Paul Schubert, Nashville, Abingdon 1966.

14. U. Wilckens, "Interpreting Paul in a Period of Existentialist Theology", in Keck and Martin, Studies in Luke-Acts, 60–83. Important insights into the extent of the influence of the apocalyptic thinking on Paul are offered by J.C. Beker, *Paul's Apocalyptic Gospel: The Coming Triumph of God*, Philadelphia, Fortress Press 1982.

15. Käsemann, *New Testament Questions of Today*, Philadelphia, Fortress Press and London, SCM Press 1969. It should be noted, however, that in another essay in this collection, Käsemann correctly draws attention to an essential feature of the New Testament – including both the gospels and Paul – namely, apocalyptic, in "On the Subject of Primitive Christian Apocalyptic", 108–37.

16. *Judaisms and Their Messiahs*, ed. J. Neusner, W.S. Green, E. Frerichs, Cambridge University Press 1987.

17. For the proposal that attention to the community setting of the New Testament writings is essential to understanding them, see my *Knowing the Truth: A Social Approach to New Testament Interpretation*, Minneapolis, Augsburg-Fortress 1989.

18. *Perspectives on Luke-Acts*, ed. Charles H. Talbert, in Special Studies Series of the Association of Baptist Professors of Religion, Danville VA. 1978. More recently, *Luke-Acts: New Perspectives*, ed. Charles H. Talbert, New York, Crossroad 1984.

19. *Political Issues in Luke-Acts*, ed. Richard J. Cassidy and P.J. Scharper, Maryknoll, New York, Orbis 1983.

20. *Luke and the People of God*, Minneapolis, Augusburg 1972. Conclusions about the relationship of the church and Israel that differ radically from Jervell's have been set forth by Jack T. Sanders in *The Jews in Luke-Acts*, Philadelphia, Fortress Press and London, SCM Press 1987. Related studies include S.G. Wilson, *Luke and the Law*, SBL Monograph Series and Robert L. Brawley, *Luke-Acts and the Jews*.

21. *Community and Gospel in Luke-Acts*, SNTS Monograph 57, Cambridge University Press 1987. Other studies of the political dimensions of Acts include Paul W. Walaskay, *"And So We Came to*

Rome": The Political Perspective of St. Luke, Cambridge University Press 1983. A collection of substantial essays on this theme is *Political Issues in Luke Acts*, ed. Cassidy and Scharper.

22. On literary dimensions of Acts see E. Pluemacher, *Lukas als hellenistischer Schriftsteller*, Göttingen 1972. On the specific links between miracle stories in Acts and those of contemporary hellenistic literature, see H.C. Kee, *Miracle in the Early Christian World*, New Haven, Yale 1983. C.H. Talbert has assessed the relationship between literary and theological factors in Acts in *Literary Patterns, Theological Themes and the Genre of Luke-Acts*, Missouls, Scholars Press 1974.

23. Ample discussion of, and documentation for this historical conclusion has been offered by Jacob Neusner in his many writings. A convenient analytical summary of his method and conclusions is offered in his *Midrash in Context*, Philadelphia, Fortress Press 1983 which is Part One: Method of a series, *The Foundations of Judaism: Method, Teleology, Doctrine*.

2. Jesus as God's Agent for Renewal of His People

1. The advanced age of the parents of Samuel and John and their inability to have a child are similar, as are the themes of the songs of Hannah and Mary in each case (Luke 1:46–55; I Sam. 2:1–10).

2. Only in Luke's version of the story of Jesus and Judas is the betrayal said to be of "the Son of Man".

3. Luke adds to the Q saying as found in Matt. 5:11 the phrase "for the sake of the son of man".

4. This is Luke's ending of the apocalyptic discourse which he has taken over basically from Mark, but which describes dramatically the degeneration of those who think themselves to be God's people and urges prayer that his hearers "may be able to stand before the Son of Man" – apparently in vindication rather than condemnation.

5. Seven times, including twice from Mark (3:22; 8:28) and twice from Q (4:5, 9).

6. All the quotations are from the LXX, which differ importantly from the Hebrew text, but the distinctive details from the LXX are in the case of the quotations from Isa. 55 and Psalm 16, essential for the argument which Paul is making.

7. Curiously, the author of Acts might have built his argument on the motifs in Isa. 55 which speak of the open invitation to the deprived and the outsiders to share in the blessings, and the new covenant which God is at work to establish. Implicitly important to the linking of these texts is the promise in Isa. 55:3 that the ground of God's action in covenant renewal is his "sure love for David."

8. In Mark 12:10–11 and Matt. 21:42, Ps. 118:22 and 23 are quoted,

but in the Lukan parallel as here in Acts 4:10, only verse 22 is quoted from the psalm.

9. Curiously the author of Acts refers to both David and Jesus as "child" or "servant" (in Greek, *pais*) designating their respective roles as agents of God for the announcement and fulfilment of the divine purpose.

10. The quotations and allusions to the prophets here have been blended and paraphrased by Acts or the tradition on which the author draws in such a way as to document from scripture the inclusion in God's people of those whose origins are outside ethnic Israel.

11. The statistics and the initial general observations are based upon Zimmerli's article in the *Theological Dictionary of the New Testament*, Vol.V, ed. G. Friedrich, trans. G.W. Bromiley, Grand Rapids, Eerdmans 1968, 654–77. In most of the remaining passages, *ebed* is rendered in Greek as *doulos*.

12. The term used of Jesus here is *hosion* (pious, righteous) in distinction from *hagios* (sacred, dedicated to God) in Acts 3:14. Both terms connote a special relationship to God, however, and stand in sharp contrast to the estimate of him by the Jewish leaders that he was evil and a threat to the integrity of God's people. The quotation from Ps. 16:10 is from the LXX and diverges considerably from the Hebrew text, which makes explicit reference to Sheol and "the Pit" as the abode of the dead. The basic point is the same, however: Jesus as the Holy One is not overcome by death.

13. Perhaps *mathetai* should be translated "learners" here, since they are incompletely taught about the resources of the life of faith, and need Paul's supplemental instruction concerning the Holy Spirit. In Chapter 5 this term is analysed in its function as a designation for the membership of the covenant community in Acts.

3. The Spirit as God's Instrument in the Present Age

1. *Pneuma* occurs in Mark 6 times; in Matthew 13 times; in Luke 17 times and in John 18, in contrast to the 58 occurrences in Acts.

2. Luke also adds to the Q saying of Jesus about God's responsiveness to prayer the promise that "the heavenly Father (will) give the Holy Spirit to those who ask him."

3. The Temple Scroll from Qumran enumerates the categories of persons who may not enter the temple. It specifically prohibits just such people (Col. 45).

4. Mark 1:8; Matt. 3:11; Luke 3:16.

5. Also known as the Feast of Weeks, or Feast of Firstfruits.

6. The dimensions and responsibilities of the early Christian fellowship are outlined repeatedly in Acts, as we shall see in dis-

cussion of the new community in Chapter 5 below. The first of these descriptions, however, follows immediately on the report of the establishment of the initial community in Jerusalem (Acts 2:43–47).

7. The financial and other arrangements for the early Christian communities as depicted in Acts are discussed below in Chapter 5.

8. The minimal requirements include abstinence from food that had been offered to idols, or from meat that was ritually impure because it contained blood or had been strangled, and from unchastity (15:20, 29). In Paul's account of his consultation with the Jerusalem leaders (Gal. 2:9–10), there were no ritual or moral obligations binding upon Gentile converts, although they were urged to offer financial help to the Jerusalem Christian community. Presumably Acts represents a later compromise position between the Jewish-Christian insistence on legal conformity, including circumcision and the dietary laws which Paul reports and his own law-free understanding of the gospel and covenantal participation as set forth in his letters.

4. Reaching Out across Religious and Cultural Boundaries

1. See Gideon Foerster, "The Art and Architecture of the Synagogue in its Late Roman Setting in Palestine" in *The Synagogue in Late Antiquity*, ed. Lee I. Levine, Philadelphia, American Schools of Oriental Research 1987, 140–46.

2. See Eric Meyers and James Strange, *Archaeology, the Rabbis and Early Christianity*, Nashville, Abingdon and London, SCM Press 1981, 81–87. They note that Bar Kochba, head of the Jewish nationalists in the Second Revolt about 130–135 CE, departs from his custom of writing to his associates in Aramaic because he is in too great a hurry and wants to be sure his readers understand fully what he is seeking to communicate. The evidence for Greek as his and their primary language is powerful.

3. Now known as Nablus.

4. Josephus, *Antiquities*, 9:288–291.

5. It is curious that neither in Acts nor in the letters of Paul is any hint offered as to how the gospel had taken root so quickly in Damascus, one of the chief hellenized cities of the Decapolis, so soon after the crucifixion of Jesus, that Saul/Paul takes such a strong initiative to stamp out the movement. One possible historical explanation of the presence and the power of the gospel there is that critical scholarship has underestimated the impact of Jesus in the Decapolis, as indicated in the gospel tradition especially in Mark (5:20; 7:31).

6. It is significant that the Gospel of Luke, while describing the ministry of Jesus in Galilee, makes the point that the ancestral home of his family was in Judaea (Bethlehem), that his earliest recorded activities occurred in Jerusalem and indeed in the temple, and all the

post-resurrection appearances of Jesus take place in the vicinity of Jerusalem as well. Ernest Lohmeyer (in *Galiläa und Jerusalem*) and R.H. Lightfoot (in *Locality and Doctrine in the Gospels*, London 1938) both assumed that there were independent streams within early Palestinian Christianity: one based in Jerusalem and the other in Galilee. In both his gospel and Acts, Luke clearly shows a special interest in locating the origins of Christianity in Jerusalem.

7. The designation of these troops as "Italian Cohort" was probably honorific and does not mean that all its soldiers were of Italian origin. At the time of the first Jewish Revolt, according to Josephus (*Wars* 2.13.7), most of those in this cohort were from Syria.

8. Several terms are used to refer to these Gentiles who remained deeply interested in Judaism even though they did not join the Jewish community: (1) *phoboumenos ton theon*, (2) *sebomenos*, and (3) *theosebes*. The first of these appears in Acts 10:2, 22, 35; 13:16, 26; the second is found in Acts 13:43, 50; 16:14; 17:4, 17; 18:7. The third has been found as an inscription at Aphrodisia in Asia Minor, which seems to prove that this term, usually translated "God-fearer", was a special designation for Gentiles who identified with Jewish beliefs but did not become members of the community. A useful discussion and bibliographical survey may be found in Gerd Luedemann, *Early Christianity according to the Traditions in Acts: A Commentary*, London, SCM Press and Philadelphia, Fortress Press 1989, 155–56.

9. H.J. Cadbury, *The Making of Luke-Acts*, London, SPCK 1927, 1961, 225.

10. II Maccabbes 6:5 describes the hellenizing program which included placing in the temple and on the altar things which according to the laws were forbidden (*athemitous*); in 7:1 people are forced to eat the forbidden pork. In III Macc. 5:20, it is the Jews themselves who are accursed and doomed for destruction by the hellenistic forces.

11. This famine-relief visit, as it is called by modern scholars, does not fit neatly into chronological schemes which have been developed for the career of Paul, nor does it seem to have a place in his account of his infrequent visits to Jerusalem in Gal. 1:18–2:10. Whether the Acts account is historical or not, it serves an important symbolic function, in that while the gospel is spreading geographically and culturally, its messengers are ever conscious of their roots in Jerusalem.

12. Mark is mentioned in the Pauline (Col. 4:10; Philemon 24), the deutero-Pauline writings (II Tim. 4:11) and is identified by "Peter" in I Peter 5:13 as "my son". It is probably the latter tradition which gave rise to the view that our oldest gospel was written by Mark.

13. Except for references to his conversion experience (Acts 22:7,

13; 26:14), Paul is not identified as Saul from this point on in the Acts narrative, but by his Greek name.

14. The opening phrase about God's returning to action is from Jer. 12:15; the central quotation is from Amos 9:11–12; the final words are a paraphrase of Isa. 45:21.

15. Quoted in translation from the Revised English Bible.

16. The crucial term, *pniktos*, does not occur in the LXX or in Jewish writing in Greek. Presumably it is an explanatory detail, showing what was essential to maintain ritual purity was killing an animal in such a way that all blood drained out, which would not be the case with strangling.

17. Martin Hengel has shown that *proseuche* was the standard term for the places where diaspora Jews gathered for a variety of purposes, including prayer and worship in "Proseuche und Synagoge", reprinted in J. Gutman (ed.), *The Synagogue: Studies in Origins, Archaeology and Architecture*, New York, Ktav 1975, 27–54. The gathered group was the *synagoge*.

18. Details in Kittel, *Theological Dictionary of the New Testament*, Grand Rapids, VIII, 614–19.

19. No evidence has been adduced concerning the altar "to an unknown god" in Athens reported in Acts beyond that already assessed by Kirsopp Lake in his 1932 note on the subject (*Beginnings of Christianity*, V, 240–46). There are literary references and possibly an inscription "to unknown gods" cited by Lake, which probably was a way of doing honor to gods in other lands whose names were not known to the Greeks. The reference in Acts is a clever literary device, whether such an inscription actually existed or not.

20. Posidonius, a native of Apamea in Syria, combined interest in the divinely ordered universe of the older Stoics with the mystical insights of the human soul in the Platonic tradition. Seneca believed that the human soul was a manifestation of the divine spirit, which should both enjoy freedom and develop discipline so that it might conform to the inherent laws of the universe. The goal of human existence is the release of the soul from the body, whereby it can escape from the conflicts of the present world. Like the earlier Stoics, both these thinkers looked forward to a new beginning in the universe. The present order would end in conflagration, all humanity would be called to account for its moral behavior, and then the creation would be renewed.

21. Set out by Wolfgang Nauck in an essay, "Die Tradition und Komposition der Areopagrede. Ein motivgeschichtliche Untersuchung", *Zeitschrift fur theologie und Kirche*, 53, 1956, 11–52. Conveniently summarized by Gerd Luedemann in *Early Christianity according to the Traditions in Acts*, 192–93.

22. The circumstances of Claudius's decree expelling the Jews

from Rome are discussed in my *What Can We Know about Jesus?*, Cambridge University Press 1990.

23. As Lily Ross Taylor has shown, the term Asiarch later became interchangeable with *Archiereus*, which was one of the priests in charge of the imperial Roman cult for the region. It probably did not have this connotation until the second century.

5. Structure and Strategy in the New Community

1. Eph. 6:21; I Tim. 3:8, 12. Anticipations of this are evident in Paul's letters: Rom. 16:1; Col. 1:7.

2. What may lie behind this account in Acts 6 of the choice of the seven with Greek names is the basic cultural and theological differences between the semitic-speaking core of the leadership based in Jerusalem and the other Christian leaders whose concern is conversion of hearers without regard to ethnic origin or ritual state. It is significant that the leadership of the Jerusalem apostles was in the hands of James the brother of Jesus, who was not a supporter of Jesus during his lifetime, if we link Mark 3:21 with 3:31–32. Surely this James was not among the twelve on any of the lists in the gospels. Peter, at the same time equivocates on the issue of the terms of the Gentile inclusion in the new community, as Paul's account in Gal. 2:11–14 makes clear. Probably this basic division among the early followers of Jesus on the issue of the terms for Gentile inclusion has been papered over by the author of Acts in this story of assigning the Greek-named group to a special role. The account of the Jerusalem council in Acts 15 pictures Paul as agreeing to a far less radical basis for Gentile inclusion than in his own account of the incident in Galatians. In Acts we hear nothing more after Acts 6 about serving tables, but we hear a great deal about the mode of *diakonia* of the word, which results in preaching and teaching and the response of faith among Gentiles.

3. The composite quotation draws on Jer. 12:15 but is primarily from Amos 9:11, with a trace of Isa. 45:21.

4. Central passages for the role of elders at crucial points in the history of ancient Israel are Ex. 24:1–11; Num. 11:16–30 and I Sam. 8:4–9.

5. The text of Acts combines the verb cognate with *synagoge* – that is *sunago* – with *ekklesia* in 14.27, thereby juxtaposing the technical terms for the Jewish and Christian community gatherings.

6. The classic depictions of women fostering illicit religious movements in the Graeco-Roman world are the *Bacchae* of Euripedes and Livy's account of the women apprehended for promoting the worship of Bacchus in 186 BCE.

7. The importance of conscience in Paul's argument in Romans

1 and 2, as well as his appeal to the law of nature, show how formative this philosophical system was in his thinking.

8. For a brief analysis of these ancient evidences of the impact of Christianity on early imperial Rome, see my *What Can We Know about Jesus?*, Cambridge University Press 1990.

6. Witnesses to the Ends of the Earth

1. The symbolic significance of the period of forty days for judgment and renewal of God's people appears across the Old Testament: the stay of Noah and those with him in the ark (Gen. 7–8); the period when Moses is alone with Yahweh on Sinai (Ex. 21:18; 31:28; Deut. 9:25); when the spies sent by Moses explore the land of Canaan (Num. 13:25; 14:34); when Elijah is with God on Mount Horeb (I Kings 19:8); when judgment is to fall on Nineveh, according to Jonah (Jonah 3:1). In each case, there is to be a major shift in the relationship of God and his people, just as is the case in the Acts narrative of Jesus' sojourn with the apostles prior to his ascension/exaltation to God's right hand.

2. Benjamin Jerome Hubbard, *The Matthean Redaction of a Primitive Apostolic Commissioning: An Exegesis of Matthew 28:16–20*, SBL Dissertation Series 19, Missoula, Montana 1974.

3. Hubbard, *Matthean Redaction*, 101–27.

4. The instances of commissioning analysed by Hubbard include the following:

Abraham: Gen. 11:28–30; 12:1–4; 15:1–6; 17:1–14
Sarah: to be the Mother of Nations; Gen. 17:15–27
Jacob: Gen. 35:9–15
Moses: Ex. 3:1–4:16
Joshua: Deut. 31:14–15, 23; Josh. 1:1–11
Samuel: I Sam. 3:1–4:1
Elijah: I Kings 19:1–19
Isaiah: Isa. 6
Jeremiah: Jer. 1:1–10
Ezekiel: Ezek. 1:1–3:15
Servant of Yahweh: Isa. 49:1–6
Solomon: by David, to build the temple; I Chron. 22:1–16

5. Hubbard, *Matthean Redaction*, 67.

6. Ibid., 122–23.

7. Benjamin Jerome Hubbard, "The Role of Commissioning Accounts in Acts", in *Perspectives on Luke-Acts*, ed. C.H. Talbert, Danville, Va. Association of Baptist Professors of Religion, 187–98. The passages from Luke-Acts analysed in this study are:

Luke 1:5–25
Luke 1:26–38

Luke 2:8–20
Luke 5:1–11
Luke 24:1–9
Luke 24:36–53
Acts 1:1–14
Acts 5:17–21a
Acts 8:26–30
Acts 9:1–9
Acts 9:10–19
Acts 10:1–8
Acts 10:30–33
Acts 11:4–12
Acts 12:6–12
Acts 13:1–3
Acts 16:8–10
Acts 18:7–11
Acts 22:6–11
Acts 22:12–16
Acts 22:17–21
Acts 23:11
Acts 26:12–20
Acts 27:21–26

8. *Hyperetes* is inadequately translated as "servant". It differs from *doulos*, "slave" or *pais*, "child" or "one who is subservient", as *diakonos*, "one to whom a duty is assigned". As Rengstorf points out in *Theological Dictionary of the New Testament*, VIII, in both classical and biblical Greek, "the special feature of *hyperetes* . . . is that he willingly learns his task and goal from another who is over him in the organic order but without prejudice to his personal dignity and worth" (533). A more accurate translation of the term would be "executive agent", who agrees to serve as plenipotentiary for a higher authority.

9. Texts reporting preaching to Jews subsequent to 13:46 include 14:1; 16:13; 17:1, 10; 18:4, 26; 19:8; 28:17, 23.

10. Still useful is the discussion and enumeration of these summaries in *The Beginnings of Christianity*, Vol.V, ed. H.J. Cadbury, who offers a literary and historical analysis, 392–402.

Index of Biblical References

OLD TESTAMENT

Genesis

9:4	59
12:6	46
22:18	22
34	46

Exodus

8:19	104

Leviticus

17:10–6	59
23:29	23

Deuteronomy

10:17	102
18	23
18:15–18	23
18:15–19	22
18:15–20	80
18:18–19	11
23:1	47

Joshua

23:32	46
24	46

Judges

9:46	46

I Samuel

13:14	16
49:6	20

I Kings

12:1	46
12:25	46
16:21–24	46
17:1; 8–9	6

18:1–2	6

II Kings

5:14	6

II Chronicles

16:35–36	103

Psalms

2	11
2:1–2	8, 16, 30
2:7	12, 14, 16
2:8–9	12
2:29–31	7
15:2	102
16:8–11	7
16:10	7, 16
16:10 (LXX)	14
69:25	15, 30, 73
89:20	16
108:9 (LXX)	79
109:8	15, 30, 71
110	32
110:1	7, 11, 15
118	18
132:11	16

Isaiah

3:26	8
4:27, 30	8
6:9–10	30, 94, 105
35:5	103
41:8–10	8
42:1	22
42:1–4	22
42:6–7	103
42:7	22
44:22	22
45:21	20. 36
49:13	22

49:5	22
49:6	56, 101
49:9	22, 103
52:13	8, 22
52:13–53	8
52:13–53:12	22
53	8, 11, 47
53:7–8	34
55:3	7, 14, 16
61	12
61:1 (LXX)	103
61:2	6
66:1–2	17, 45

Jeremiah

12:15	20, 36

Daniel

7:13–14	8
7:18, 22	8

Joel

2:16	31, 100
2:17–21	31
2:21	32
2:28–30	9
3:1	80
3:1–5	31

Amos

5:25–27	45
9:11 (LXX)	59
9:11–12	17, 20, 36
9:12 (LXX)	59

Habakkuk

1:5	8, 24, 55

Malachi

5:5–6	23

NEW TESTAMENT

Matthew

12:15–21	22
13:57	22
16:14	23
21:33–46	18
28:16–20	98

Mark

1:32–34	14
2:23–28	15
5:7	62
6:1–6	29
6:4	22
6:15	22
8:28	23
9:2–8	33
10:33	13
10:47–48	15
12:1–12	18
12:35–37	15
14:62	13
16:7	13

Luke

1:27	15
1:32	14
1:35	28
1:36	62
1:41	28
1:54	22
1:69	22
1:76	62
2:1–20	88
2:4	15
2:11	15
2:25–27	28
2:33	88
2:36	88
2:51	88
3:22	28
3:31	15
4:16–21	6, 12, 29
4:25–28	6
4:41	14
6:1–5	15
6:5	13
6:22	13
6:35	62
7:11–17	88
7:16	23
7:34	13
7:36–50	88
8:1–3	88
8:6	88
8:28	62
9:8	22
9:19	23

9:22	13
9:26	13
9:44	13
9:58	13
11:20	104
11:27–28	88
13:10–17	88
13:33	23
15:8–10	88
16:16	3
16:31	23
17:20, 24, 26, 30	13
18:8	13
18:31	13
18:38–39	15
19:10	13
20:9–19	18
20:41–44	15
21:27, 36	13
22:22	13
22:29–30	71
22:48	13
22:69	13
22:70	14
24:19	23
24:26	13
24:26–27, 44	7
24:27, 45	71
24:36–53	99
24:44	99
24:45–47	99
24:47	89
24:48	89, 96

John

1:21	23
4:46	23
7:40	23

Acts

1–8	96
1:1–14	99
1:2	36, 71
1:2–3	9
1:4	42
1:4–5	36
1:5	30
1:6	20, 100
1:8	30, 71, 75
1:9–11	100
1:14	87
1:15	86
1:15–20	30
1:15–26	79
1:16	16
1:17	78
1:20	14, 71

1:21	20
1:21–22	9
1:22	71
1:24	19
1:25	78
2	31, 42
2:1–2	31
2:3	31
2:7	31
2:7–11	31
2:8	72
2:10	6, 26, 32
2:14–36	89
2:17	80
2:19	9
2:23	9
2:25	21
2:25–28	7, 16
2:29	83
2:31	11
2:22	9, 92
2:32–36	11
2:33	26, 28
2:34	21
2:34–35	7
2:34–36	16
2:36	32
2:37	83
2:38	24, 32
2:39	19, 24
2:41	32, 81, 106
2:41–47	86
2:42	72
2:43	9
2:44	81
2:46	87, 88
2:47	20, 106
3	18, 70
3:11–26	26, 89
3:12	21
3:13	8, 21
3:14–16	23
3:15	26, 96
3:16	9
3:17–24	80
3:18	8
3:18–20	11
3:19	27
3:19–22	19
3:20–23	22
3:20–26	70
3:21	27
3:24–26	22
3:25–26	80
3:26	21, 22
4:1–7	37
4:1–22	11
4:2	72, 89, 90

Acts (cont.)

4:4	72, 81
4:5	42
4:8–10	37
4:10	18
4:10–11	18
4:10–12	72
4:13	72
4:16–18	9
4:18	90
4:20	72
4:21	9
4:23ff	87
4:23–28	16
4:25–26	11
4:25–27	73
4:25–28	30
4:27–31	37
4:28	73
4:31	72, 73
4:32	81
4:32–37	87
4:33	21, 89, 96
5	44
5:1–11	87
5:1–32	33
5:3	39
5:5	39
5:7–10	39
5:9	20
5:11	84
5:12	43
5:12–16	9, 87
5:14	21, 81, 87
5:17–21	73, 90
5:19–20	40
5:25	90
5:27–42	43
5:28	26, 90
5:30–31	89
5:30–32	26
5:31	26
5:32	86
5:33–39	74
5:39	43
5:40–42	74
5:42	43, 88, 90
6	33, 72, 77
6:1	85
6:1–3	33
6:1–6	9, 43
6:2	72, 74
6:2–3	73
6:4	72, 74
6:5	33, 44
6:6	77
6:7	72, 85, 106
6:8	10, 77
6:9	44
6:9–11	44

6:10	77
7	32, 33, 74
7:2	44, 83
7:4–5	45
7:9–16	45
7:30–41	45
7:31–33	19
7:34–35	71
7:37	23
7:38	84
7:42–43	45
7:43	45
7:45–48	45
7:49–50	45
5:51	24, 34, 39
7:51–53	45
7:52	23, 24
7:52–53	24
7:55	33
7:55–56	27, 77
7:56	13
7:57	88
7:59	21
7:60	20
8	32
8:1	46, 74, 84, 85
8:2	51
8:3	88
8:4–7	47, 73, 75
8–4:8	77
8:4–5	89
8:5	34
8:6	10
8:7	10
8:9–11	39
8:9–24	10
8:12	81
8:12–13	25, 40, 77
8:14	73
8:16–17	34
8:17	71
8:18–19	39
8:18–24	34
8:21–23	40
8:24	20, 40
8:25	47, 73, 75
8:26	40
8:26–30	100
8:26–40	47
8:27–34	34
8:32–33	8
8:32–35	50
8:35	100
8:36–43	50
8:39–40	34
9:1	21, 85
9:1–3	49
9:1–9	100
9:2	49
9:10	86

9:10–19	100
9:10–11	21
9:11	48
9:13	21, 85
9:14	25
9:15	21, 25, 49, 50
9:17	21, 34
9:20	14, 89
9:21	49
9:22	49
9:23	49
9:25	86
9:26, 27	75
9:29	49
9:30	83
9:31	50, 85, 106
9:35	21
9:38	86
9:42	21
10	29, 34, 77
10:1–8	101
10:2	5, 89
10:3–7	40
10:4	20
10:9–23	101
10:17	51
10:20	52
10:22	40, 52
10:23	84
10:26	21, 86
10:28	52, 102
10:29	86
10:33	20
10:34–35	102
10:34–43	12
10:36	53, 71, 73
10:38	29
10:39	53, 97
10:40	97
10:40–42	29
10:42	27, 87, 89
10:43	53, 81, 102
10:44	53, 73
10:44–48	25
10:45	34
10:47–48	34
11:1	53, 73
11:1–16	75
11:2–3	53
11:9	53
11:12	35, 53, 84
11:13	40
11:14	89
11:15–16	35
11:16	21
11:17	21, 53, 75, 82
11:18	53, 75
11:19	73
11:19–20	35, 54
11:19–21	44

Acts (cont.)		14:4	77	16:14–15	20
11:21	24, 82, 106	14:8–18	10, 57	16:15	89
11:24	21, 35, 54, 106	14:15–17	57	16:16–18	102
11:25	90	14:15–18	92	16:17	61
11:25–26	54, 73	14:20	86	16:18	62
11:26	35, 85	14:21	57, 86	16:20–21	62
11:27	78	14:21–22	57	16:22–23	62
11:28	37	14:23	79	16:25–26	102
11:29	78	14:27	75	16:25–27	62
11:30	37	14:28	86	16:30–31	62
12:1–2	54	15	3, 35, 57, 75, 90	16:31	21, 82
12:1ff	85	15:1	58, 76, 84	16:32–34	62
12:1–10	40	15:2	58, 76	16:34	82
12:2–17	54	15:3	58	16:35–40	62
12:5	85	15:3–4	36, 76	17	48, 57, 91
12:11	20	15:4	78, 85	17:1–9	57
12:12	54	15:4–5	58	17:6	84
12:17	20, 83	15:5	35, 82	17:10	84
12:20	88	15:5–6	76	17:10–15	63
12:20–23	41	15:6	78	17:12	82
12:24	73, 106	15:6–11	76	17:18	84
12:25	78	15:7	82	17:22	64
13	100	15:7–8	36	17:24	64
13:1	80	15:8	35	17:25–26	64
13:1–2	35	5:10	58, 86	17:27–28	64
13:1–3	54	15:10–11	36	17:28	64
13:2	21	15:11	58	17:29–30	64
13:5–6	55	15:12	10, 17, 58, 76	17:31	27, 64
13:7–12	40	15:12–18	36	17:34	82
13:8	55	15:13	83	18:1–4	65
13:9	35	15:13–18	20	18:1–20	93
13:12	82	15:16–18	17	18:6	65
13:13–41	55	15:17	59	18:7	88
13:16–22	16	15:18	59	18:7–8	66
13:16–23	7	15:21	59	18:8	82, 89
13:20	20	15:22	60, 78, 81	18:9	21
13:23	85	15:22–29	76, 85	18:9–10	41
13:26	83	15:23	78, 83	18:11	91
13:26–39	14	15:24–26	25	18:12	88
13:27–28	24	15:25	88	18:12–17	66
13:30	9	15:28	36, 76	18:18	66, 84
13:31	97	15:30–34	76	18:19	66
13:32	7	15:32	60, 81	18:23	86
13:33	16	15:32–33	84	18:24–27	91
13:33–35	7	15:35	76	18:24–28	66
13:35	16, 17, 24	15:36	84	18:27	84
13:38	14, 83	15:36–16:5	37	19:1	86
13:40–41	8	15:40	84	19:1–6	25, 66
13:41	24, 55, 82	16	60	19:2	81
13:43	56	16:1–3	60	19:8	66
13:44–45	56	16:2	84	19:8–10	66
13:47	21, 56, 101, 107	16:4	78	19:9	86, 88
13:48	82	16:4–5	60	19:11–20	66
13:51	56	16:5	106	19:13	90
13:52	86	16:6–7	37	19:20	106
14	10	16:8	38	19:21	38
14:1	82	16:9	41	19:29	88
14:1–7	10, 56	16:10	41	19:31	67
14:2	84	16:11–13	61	19:32	84
14:3	21	16:14	61	19:39	84

Acts (cont.)

20:1	86
20:17	38
20:17–18	85
20:17–35	79
20:18	78, 85
20:19	2, 38
20:20–26	66
20:21	21, 38
20:22–23	38
20:24	78, 97
20:25	90
20:28–32	79
20:28	85
20:30	86
20:32	73
21:4	38, 86
21:7	84
21:7–12	25
21:9	81
21:10	81
21:13	21, 25, 39
21:14	20, 39
21:16	86
21:18	78
21:19	78
21:20	82
21:25	76, 82
21:27	67
21:28	67
21:35	67
21:37–40	25
22:1–5	67
22:3	48
22:4	49
22:5	83
22:6–16	102

22:12	102
22:12–16	25
22:14	102
22:14–14	97
22:21	50
22:25–29	67
22:30	67
23:3	67
23:6–9	67
23:11	21, 97
24:14	49, 82
24:25	68
24:47	89
24:48	89
25:8–12	68
25:13–26	68
25:21	68
26:9	25
26:9–11	49
26:10	85
26:12–20	102
26:16–18	97
26:17	71
26:18	103
26:19–23	68
26:21–23	23
26:27	82
26:31	68
26:32	68
27:21–25	41
27:21–26	104
27:24	68
27:25	82
27:43	68
28:1–6	68
28:14	84
28:15	84

28:16	68, 92
28:17–18	92
28:19	68
28:19–20	69
28:21	83
28:23	97
28:23–28	68, 105
28:25–27	30, 94
28:25–28	97
28:28	69, 71, 94
28:30	92
28:30–31	107
28:31	21, 90

Romans

16:3	93

I Corinthians

12:10	31
14:1–19	31
15:20	11

Galatians

1:11–17	49
1:18–23	49
1:23	49
2:1–10	60

I Timothy

5	79

Hebrews

12:2	26

I Peter

1:1	38
2:12	79
4:3	52

APOCRYPHA

Sirach

35:12	102

NON-CANONICAL

Dead Sea Scrolls

The Messianic Anthology 1Q Sa	11	The Messianic Rule 4Q 175	11

Jubilees

7:34–37	30	15:1–16	30
14:1–6	30	22:1–9	30